A

SLOW

The Kingdom Express

COMING

God's Redemptive Plan for Israel and the Church

**An anthology of seminar messages by
David Silver**

A SLOW  COMING

A SLOW TRAIN COMING
by David Silver

Published by Out of Zion Ministries
Mt. Carmel
Israel
www.out-of-zion.com

A Slow Train Coming
ISBN 81-87858-56-7

3rd Edition August 2003
2000/JS

Contents

A SLOW COMING

Part 2: Israel - Present and Future

A SLOW COMING

About the Author

David Silver is the founder/director of **OUT OF ZION** Ministries, based on Mt. Carmel in Haifa, Israel. David was born in Auckland, New Zealand. He was radically 'born-again' in April 1987. In 1992 he sensed the Lord calling him to leave New Zealand and take his wife Josie, and their two sons, Stefan and Jordan, to return to the land of his forefathers.

The Silver family now lives on Mt. Carmel and are founding members of Tents of Mercy Congregation in Haifa Bay. **OUT of ZION** Ministries function under the oversight of the Tents of Mercy leadership team. In 1995 David and Josie became involved in Jewish evangelism, they travelled to Moscow to participate in an outreach to the Jewish residents of that city. Then followed similar events in Moldova and Latvia. While in Latvia, the Lord spoke to David and placed the vision for **OUT of ZION** Ministries firmly in his heart.

Initially the vision was to fulfil the scripture in Isaiah 2:3 *For Out of Zion shall go forth the Law and the Word of the Lord from Jerusalem;* to fulfil God's call on Israel as His Chosen Nation to be a light to the nations; to encourage and facilitate sending out teams of Israelis to the nations, specifically those with large Jewish communities; to take the Word of the Lord to the Jew first and also to the Gentiles.

Within a few weeks of establishing **OUT of ZION** Ministries David and fellow Jewish evangelist Jeff Bernstein found themselves working together under the oversight of Tents of Mercy Congregation, organising and administrating Jewish outreach festivals in the Russian cities of Samara and Murmansk.

A SLOW COMING

As they travelled the vast distances and encountered many difficulties working in the former USSR the Lord again spoke to David and showed him that He had in fact called the Gentiles to assist Him in bringing the Jewish people back to Israel and that it was His plan for the Church to provoke the Jewish people to return to their God. (Romans 11:11)

David continues to have a strong vision for Jewish evangelism, but has also embarked on a course of endeavouring to teach the Church about her Jewish roots and her relationship and responsibility to Israel and the Jewish people.

David now travels extensively conducting seminars and speaking to churches and prayer groups about the Biblical relationship between Israel and the Church, in the hope of awakening Christians to the prophetic relevance of Israel's rebirth and the calling on the Gentile Christians to co-labour with the Lord as He completes the restoration of Israel in preparation for the second coming of the Messiah.

David is also fulfilling his calling as an evangelist to the nations and has preached an 'Israel centred' Gospel message in Samoa, India, Kenya and Malaysia.

****

Dedication

This book is dedicated to the memory of millions of Jewish men, women and children, and the millions of true Christians, reborn by the Spirit of God, who have perished over the last two millennia at the unmerciful, unloving hands of those who also claimed the Son of the God, Yeshua the Jewish Messiah, as their Lord and Saviour, but having been deceived by the evil one, took it upon themselves to be judge, jury and many times, executioner.

A SLOW COMING

Acknowledgements

I wish to acknowledge the following people who have all been a part of the realization of this book

- My wife Josie and our sons, Stefan and Jordan, for releasing and blessing me to travel to the many different nations that the Lord has opened before us.

- Josie for her faithful prayer support and intercession for the ministry that the Lord has called us to.

- The men of God who have been preaching the truth about Israel for more than thirty years now. Men like Derek Prince, Lance Lambert and David Pawson were 'pioneers' of the pro-Israel movement and have been a source of much inspiration to me.

- My pastor Eitan Shishkoff for his leadership and apostolic example, and fellow Kiwi / Israeli Evan Thomas, who with his wife Maala, prayed us through the initial years of our Aliyah.

- Our wonderful and incredible intercessors. Men and women in many different countries who, through their faithful prayer and material support, are an integral part of **Out of Zion** Ministries.

- Last but definitely not least, the God of Israel who has blessed our family with the awesome privilege of serving Him in His Holy Land and in the nations, at such a time as this.

A SLOW  COMING

Hebrew / English Glossary

Yeshua	Jesus
Elohim	God
Adonai	Lord
Messiah	Christ or Anointed One
Tenach	Old Testament
Brit Hadashah	New Testament

Suggested Reading List

Our Hands Are Stained With Blood   Dr. M Brown
Destiny Image   ISBN 1-56043-068-0

Hastening the Day of His Coming   Johanas Facias
Sovereign World International   ISBN 1-85240-298-9

Your People Shall be My People   Pastor Don Finto
Regal Books   ISBN 0-8307-2653-5

The Last Word on the Middle East   Derek Prince
Chosen Books   ISBN   0-310-60040-5

Philistine   Ramon Bennett
Arm of Salvation   ISBN 965-90000-1-4

Introduction

Author's Preface

Acts 4:33 *And with **<u>great power the apostles</u>** gave witness to the resurrection of the Lord Jesus.*

Acts 5:12-16 *And through the hands of the apostles, many signs and wonders were done among the people.... so that they brought the sick out into the streets and laid them on beds and couches that at least the **<u>shadow of Peter</u>** passing might fall on some of them. Also a multitude gathered from the surrounding cities to Jerusalem bringing sick people and those who were tormented by unclean spirits and **<u>all were healed</u>**.*

John 14:12 *Most assuredly I say to you, he who believes in Me, the works that I do he will do also; and **<u>greater works</u>** than these he will do.* Is this a picture of your life, your ministry, or the life of your church? In the majority our answer must be 'unfortunately not'. Something has gone very **WRONG.**

Sadly, most of our lives, and the life we see in the various streams of Christianity, for the most part do not display the dynamic power that was once seen in the ministry of the early church. The objective of this book is to create a hunger in the reader, to seek a return to those exciting times.

This book is not intended to be negative or critical, but through looking closely at historical events and relative scriptures, address the reality of modern Church life, and the reasons

A SLOW  COMING

for the loss of the miracle working power, last seen on a daily basis, in the Church of the first century.

We will also study one of the most ignored and/or misunderstood subjects in Christendom - **God's last day plans and purposes for Israel and the Church.**

My hope is that this will inspire each of us to sow our lives into the effort to bring about the restoration of God's design for Israel and the Church, as both entities rise up to become one people, serving the God of Israel. It is my belief that this restoration will result in the restoration of the full power of the Holy Spirit to the Body of Messiah.

****

The Days of Elijah

The following song has made an impact upon the Body of Messiah as it has been sung in churches around the world. The Bible tells us that God will send the prophet Elijah before that great and awesome day of the Lord's coming. I believe that heaven has given us this anointed song specifically for the time in which we live. The lyrics of this song encompass the message that **OUT OF ZION** Ministries endeavours to bring to the Church in these exciting end-times.

These are the days of Elijah
Declaring the Word of the Lord
And these are the days of Your servant Moses
Righteousness being restored
And these are the days of great trials
Of famine and darkness and sword
Still we are the voice in the desert crying
"Prepare ye the way of the Lord"

chorus: *Behold He comes riding on the clouds*
Shining like the sun at the trumpet call
So lift your voice - it's the year of jubilee
Out of Zion's hill salvation comes

And these are the days of Ezekiel
The dry bones becoming as flesh
And these are the days of Your servant David
Rebuilding the temple of praise
And these are the days of the harvest
The fields are white in the world
And we are Your labourers in Your vineyard
Declaring the Word of the Lord

copyright : Robin Marks

15

A SLOW  COMING

A Prophetic Word Concerning Israel and the Church
- Rick Joyner 1987

In his book 'The Harvest' Rick Joyner shares a prophetic vision of end time events that he was given in 1987. I quote from chapter six entitled `Israel and the Church' -

"There will be a time of increasing controversy in the Church about the place of Israel and Jews in the plan of God. This

contention will polarise much of the church into extreme positions. These positions will basically consist of those who will see only the 'natural' Jew and the nation of Israel, and God's purpose to close the end of the age and bring in the end time harvest, and those who only see 'spiritual Israel', the Church, which is composed of those who are Jews after the spirit, as having a purpose in the plan of God for this day. The enemy will try to make it one of the most divisive questions confronting the last day Church. Satan is not targeting this just because it is convenient, but because the Church's proper understanding of this issue will be essential if she is to accomplish her end time mandate.

Satan has historically caused such a controversy before the restoration of every important truth to the Church. Ultimately this contention will result in a more clear revelation to the whole Body of Christ on this important and timely truth. .... Because of the ultimate significance of this truth to God's purposes, Satan will soon be releasing every demon in hell to divide the Church over these issues and to bring enmity between Christians and Jews."

****

We Need to Pray

What you are about to read, you may have never seen or heard before. To some readers the message of this book may seem very radical. The implications of this message are so important, that the truth concerning Israel must come to you by revelation of the Holy Spirit and the Word of God.

Every person who is a part of the true Church of Yeshua the Messiah has a Biblical relationship and thus a responsibility to the Jewish people and the nation of Israel. Satan has done an incredible job of deceiving the Church out of this relationship with Israel, and she has not fulfilled her responsibility to Israel since the end of the first century when the doctrine of Replacement Theology entered the Church. Romans chapter 11 tells us that "blindness in part has come upon the Jews", but surely, the other part of the blindness has come upon the Church.

If we truly are living at the end of the age, then just as God is lifting the veil that blinds the Jewish people to the truth of the Messiah, I believe He is also in the process of taking the veil off the Church, so that she may rise up and fulfil her destiny to join the Royal Priesthood and to fulfil her calling to 'provoke the Jewish people to jealousy'.

God of Abraham, Isaac and Jacob, I bind every lying and deceiving spirit that would attempt to blind the reader to Your truth. Holy Spirit, I ask You to anoint the message of this book, so that whether it is being heard or read, there will be a spirit of revelation of truth upon it, and that Your people will know the truth and the truth will set them free.
In Yeshua's name   - Amen!

A SLOW COMING

Part 1:

A History of Israel and the Church

A SLOW COMING

Chapter 1

A Slow Train Coming

Not Israel Just For Israel's Sake

Israel is the key to church unity and world redemption

The central subject of this book, the relationship and responsibility of the Church to Israel and the Jewish people, is guaranteed to spark a heated debate, and ultimately may be the issue that will separate the true Church from the apostate church.

Many Gentile Christians have not been able to come to terms with the fact that God still has a special place for the Jewish people, let alone that they could still be referred to as 'the chosen people'.

Before I go any further, I want to reassure my Gentile readers that the Jewish race was born for the sake of the rest of the world. Chosen they were, and chosen they still are, to be a *Holy nation, a Royal Priesthood* (Exodus 19:6), to be His representatives to *bless all of the nations of the earth* (Genesis 12:2, 18:18, 26:4,28:14) and to be *a light to the nations* (Isaiah 49:6). Israel's 'choseness' is for the sake of the rest of the world, for God so loves the world, that He created the nation of Israel to work with Him, to redeem all of the others nations.

The 'return from the dead' of the secular nation of Israel in 1948, and the ever increasing number of Jews coming to faith in Messiah since 1967, has awesome implications for the entire Church, and the whole world. We will see the actual statistics in the chapter entitled "Times of Restoration". Such numbers of Jewish people coming to faith in Yeshua, have not been seen since the early days of the Church in the first century. It is a sovereign work of God

Since early in the 2nd century, there has been much controversy in the Church concerning Israel and the Jewish people and particularly the Jewish believers. This has been a direct attack of the Devil in an attempt to hinder God's plans and purposes for the Jewish people.

It is imperative in these last days that we all understand and embrace the role of Israel and align ourselves with the Lord, as He brings His plans and purposes to fulfilment.

The Lord has two specific roles for Israel in these last days.

1/ Israel is the key to Church unity.

The first major split in the Church came after the rejection of the Jewish believers by the Gentile believers, after the Messianic Jews had embraced the Gentiles and did not require them to become Jewish (Acts 15).

Once the Gentile Christians separated themselves from the Jewish believers and her Biblical roots, claiming that the Church had now replaced Israel, it was easy for subsequent groups to also separate and claim that they were now the 'chosen ones'.

This cycle of separation, and claiming to be the group that God is now dealing with, has continued down through the last 1900 years of Church history and the fruit of it is that we have hundreds of denominations and thousands of variations within these denominations. The most extreme separations have resulted in cults like the Mormons and Jehovah's Witnesses.

The Kingdom of Heaven is coming, and I am sure that Heaven will not be divided into denominations. Nor for that matter, will there be a separate Heaven for Jews and Christians. Now is the time for all believers to become one in the one Messiah.

I totally agree with a born-again spirit-filled Catholic priest, Father Peter Hocken, who wrote in his book "The Glory and the Shame", that *the Church will only become one body again, not by all believers returning to one particular denomination, but as more and more denominations are awakened and reconciled to the Jewish roots, all denominations will be reconciled in a unified theology.*

When all of the denominations return to a Biblically based theology, all of the differences will disappear, and we will truly be one in Word and deed. When the Church is restored to her Biblical roots, the relationship between Jewish and Gentile believers will also be restored.

The fruit of this will be revival to the powerful anointing of the early Church that many are crying out for.

A SLOW  COMING

Rom 11:15 *For if their being cast away is the reconciling of the world, what will their acceptance be but **life from the dead?***

What else is '**life from the dead**', but **REVIVAL?**

2/ Israel - The key to world redemption

Isaiah 11:11 - 12 *It shall come to pass in that day that the LORD shall set His hand again the second time to recover the remnant of His people who are left, from Assyria and Egypt, from Pathros and Cush, from Elam and Shinar, from Hamath and the islands of the sea. He will set up a banner for the nations, and will assemble the outcasts of Israel, and gather together the dispersed of Judah from the four corners of the earth.*

The Lord tells us that when He brings back the Jews a second time, this time from all over the world, it will be for a banner to the nations. What is a banner? A banner is a large sign. God is using the restoration of Israel as a sign to the whole world.

We see many banners or signs out there in our towns and cities. Signs for popular soft drinks, new cars, movies etc. So what does this sign from God to the nations say? Perhaps it says something like this ....

"This is God calling Earth. I am not dead !" (most people live today as if they think God died in the late 60's) *I am alive and at work in the world today. Look at what I am doing with Israel. It's a sign to you, a sign that my Son is about to return to Earth. Are you ready?"*

And if the world still doesn't take notice, once the Jews are back in their land and back in a right relationship with God by way of the blood of the Messiah, He will then send them out, 144,000 of them according to Revelation 7:4 and 14:1, to finally fulfil that call to be *'light to the nations'*. 144,000 Jewish evangelists who will sing a *new song, the song of Moses and the song of the Lamb.* (Revelation 15:3)

Finally the prophecies and the great commission will be completed and there will be a worldwide revival

Isaiah 11:9-12 .... *for the earth shall be full of the knowledge of the LORD as the waters cover the sea.*

The real purpose that the Lord chose Israel is to bring His Salvation to the world, but it is not as straight forward as that. Israel fell and most of the natural branches have been broken off, making way for the Gentiles to be grafted into the Olive tree. But the Lord tells us in Romans 11:24–30, that He is more than able to regraft the natural branches back in, that the gifts and calling He gave them is irrevocable, and that ultimately, all Israel will be saved. That momentous event will open the way for the 144,000 Jewish evangelists who will embark on the final harvest ....

And then the end will come !

Read on and we will take a closer look at this amazing story..............

A SLOW COMING

Major Events in Israel's History

BC Events
* **2166** Abram Born
* **2060** God makes covenant with Abraham (Gen 12:3)
* **1446** The Exodus   (Exodus 12:51)
* **1406** Israelites enter Canaan
* **586** Fall of Jerusalem
* **597-527** Babylonian Exile
* **538-432** First Restoration
* **180-175** Antiochus Epiphanes and the Macabee Revolt

AD Events
* **   ** Yeshua Born   (Matthew 1:25)
* **26** Yeshua's ministry begins
* **30** Crucifixion. Resurrection and Ascension
* **70-135** Second Temple destroyed, Jerusalem
     sacked and second Jewish dispersion
* **1897** First Zionist Conference at Basel - Switzerland
* **1917** General Allenby liberates Jerusalem
* **1947** United Nations grants Israel statehood
* **1948** May 14th Israel officially becomes a nation
     (Ezekiel 36:8 and Isaiah 66:8)
     Arab nations declare war
* **1967** Six Day War, Jerusalem reunited after 1900 yrs
* **1967** Re-birth of Messianic Church (Hosea 3:5 and
     Jeremiah 30:9)
* **1973** Yom Kippur War
* **???** Yeshua returns to Jerusalem to reign for 1000
     years

****

6000 Years of History

Several years ago many Christians in the West placed a bumper sticker on their automobiles. The sticker read "ONE WAY JESUS". We should all be able to agree with that sticker. There is only one way that leads to the Father. There is only one plan of salvation that will ultimately lead on to eternal life with the One True God, the God of Israel.

I felt inspired to produce the 'Slow Train Coming' railway map on the following page, to be used as a visual aid to clearly show the plan for world redemption that God has been working out over the last six thousand years of history. I wonder, is it just a coincidence that, in English, that word is made up by two syllables - **His Story** ?

Travel with me on the "Slow Train" as we travel through six thousand years, on the only track that leads to salvation.

Every event in the Bible and many events that have occurred over the last 6000 years are stations on the 'Slow Train' railway. However we will only be looking at the major stations on the track. These dramatic events have shaped Israel's history and, whether the other nations in the world realize it or not, Israel's history has shaped world history. The world's greatest empires have risen and fallen in respect to their treatment of Israel and the Jewish people.

The 'Slow Train Coming' map portrays 6000 years of history giving a very clear picture of the tumultuous events that have shaped life on planet Earth. Though tragically, millions of men, women and children have perished in the many wars that have been fought along the way, there is a day coming when "*Swords will be beaten into plowshares.*"

A SLOW  COMING

God's Plan For World Redemption – A 'One Track' Plan

> John 4:22 For Salvation is of the Jews (Jesus speaking)
> Rom 11:17 And if some of the branches were broken off,
> and you, being a wild olive tree, were grafted in among
> them, and with them became a partaker of the root and
> fatness of the olive tree

The Nations
(on the wrong tracks)

God's One Track Plan of Salvation

*	*	*	*
Adam & Eve	**Abraham**	**The Exodus**	**Calling to the Nations**
Gen 2 & 3	**Gen 12:3**	**Ex 12**	**Ex 19:6**

Gen 12:1-3 Now the LORD had said to Abram: "Get out of your country, from your family and from your father's house, to a land that I will show you. I will make you a great nation; I will bless you and make your name great; and you shall be a blessing. I will bless those who bless you, and I will curse him who curses you; and in you all the families of the earth shall be blessed."

Ex 12:51 And it came to pass on that same day that the Lord brought the children of Israel out of the Land of Egypt

Matt 1:25 And she brought forth her firstborn Son and called His name Yeshua

Acts 3:21 "whom heaven must receive until the times of restoration of all things, which God has spoken by the mouth of all His holy prophets since the world began.

Ez 36: 8 O mountains of Israel, you shall shoot forth your branches and yield your fruit to my people Israel, for they are about to come

From Adam to the Second Coming of Messiah

By David Silver

The Kingdom Express

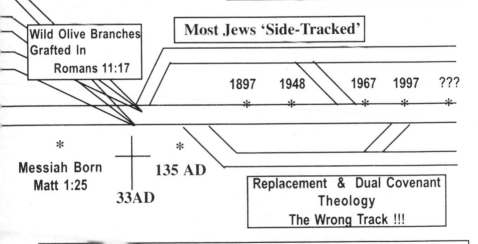

**Wild Olive Branches Grafted In
Romans 11:17**

Most Jews 'Side-Tracked'

1897   1948   1967   1997   ???

*   *
**Messiah Born
Matt 1:25**   **135 AD**

33AD

**Replacement & Dual Covenant
Theology
The Wrong Track !!!**

Ez 37:4 Prophesy to those dry bones and say to them "hear the word of the Lord" ....

Ez 37:9 Come from the four winds O breath and breathe on these slain that they may live

Hosea 3:5 Afterward the children of Israel shall return and seek the Lord their God & **David their King**

Isaiah 2:3 For Out of Zion shall go forth the Torah and the Word of the Lord from Jerusalem

Rev 1:7 Behold He is coming with the clouds and every eye shall see Him even they who pierced Him

A SLOW ⬛ COMING

The Main Stations on the Slow Train Track

4000 BC The Garden of Eden

In Genesis chapter 1, we read of the fall of man. The serpent deceives Adam and Eve into eating the only forbidden fruit. Adam and Eve are separated from God by their sin and are cast out of the Garden. However, God has a plan to redeem mankind back to Himself - the Slow Train is on its journey.

2060 BC Abrahamic Covenant

God chooses a man called Abram and enters into an eternal land covenant with him (Genesis 12 -15). Abram's name is changed to Abraham. Abraham is instructed to leave his home and family and make his way to a place that God would show him. God promises Abraham that one day his descendants will be a great nation to be a blessing to the other nations. And so the incredible history of the Jewish people begins. Abraham's family are on the train.

1446 BC The Exodus

The descendants of Abraham now number in the millions, but they are slaves to the cruel Pharaoh in Egypt and God hears their cries. The set time arrives for their deliverance from slavery and God chooses another man, Moses, to be His servant to set His people free. The Pharaoh resists and God is forced to show His power. After the slaying of the first born sons of the Egyptians, Pharaoh agrees to let God's people go. However he again changes his mind, a big mistake, and his army is drowned in the Red Sea after the Israelites pass through on the way to the promised land.

31

A SLOW  COMING

1446 BC Mt Sinai

Moses leads the Israelites through the desert. Arriving at Mt. Sinai, Moses is summoned up to the top of the mountain, where God gives the Jewish people His instructions for survival – the Torah.

Here at Mt.Sinai, the Lord also pronounces Israel's destiny.

Exodus19:6 *'And you shall be to Me a kingdom of priests and a holy nation.'*

The Birth of the Messiah

Almost 1500 years later, the Lord is set to reveal His arm once again. The Jewish people have had a chequered history, often failing to fulfil their destiny as a Royal Priesthood. The set time arrives for the Messiah, the Lamb of God, to enter the world scene, via Israel and the Jewish people.

Isaiah 9:6-7 *For unto us a child is born, unto us a son is given: and the government shall be upon his shoulder: and his name shall be called Wonderful, Counsellor, The Mighty God, The everlasting Father, The Prince of Peace. Of the increase of his government and peace there shall be no end, upon the throne of David,*

The Death and Resurrection of Yeshua

Yeshua the Messiah ministers the Word of God to the Jewish people for 3 years, before the dramatic events, that were ordained from the foundation of the world, begin to unfold.

At the time of the Passover, a Holy feast which remembers the Exodus from Egypt and foreshadows the deliverance from sin for Israel and the nations, Yeshua the Lamb of God, becomes a 'corban', a sacrifice, that His blood would cleanse us of our sin and seal the New Covenant prophesied hundreds of years earlier by the prophet Jeremiah.

Jeremiah 31:31-32 *"Behold, the days are coming, says the LORD, when I will make a new covenant with the house of Israel and with the house of Judah—not according to the covenant that I made with their fathers in the day that I took them by the hand to lead them out of the land of Egypt, My covenant which they broke, though I was a husband to them, says the LORD."*

AD 135 Replacement Theology

Paul warned the Church to *"beware of wolves in sheep's clothing"* (Acts 20:29). I believe this was a warning about the false doctrine which entered the Church early in the 2nd century and was taught by many of the men who are today acknowledged as 'the Church fathers'. They began to teach that God had eternally finished dealing with Israel and the Church was now solely the Israel of God. This is not what the Bible says

Romans 11:1 *I say then, has God cast away His people?* ***Certainly not !***

Unfortunately for the next 1900 years this theology has been the foundation of much of Church theology and today is rampant in many Church denominations in the world. It is known as Replacement Theology, and we will take a closer look at this in chapter 4.

A SLOW  COMING

1897 The First Zionist Congress

The Jewish people had been persecuted since they were scattered to the nations 1900 years earlier. They had been rounded up, contained in ghettos, and often falsely accused of crimes against Christians. As punishment they were tormented and many times killed in significant numbers.

The 'straw that broke the camel's back' was the Dreyfus trial in France in the late 19th century. The false accusation and subsequent trial of this Jewish French army officer inspired leaders of the European Jewish communities to begin to meet together, to bring about the restoration of a Jewish homeland.

The first meeting of the Zionists was held in 1897 in Basel, Switzerland. These Zionist leaders were not religious, but I believe that they were being inspired by the Holy Spirit, as the appointed time for Psalm 102:13 to be fulfilled arrived.

Psalm 102:13 *You will arise and have mercy on Zion; for the time to favour her, yes, the set time, has come.*

The time of the Lord's return took a big step forward!

Psalm 102:16 *For the LORD shall build up Zion; he shall appear in His glory.*

1948   Israel Becomes a Nation

God was at work through the two world wars. The face of Europe changed as He prepared for the greatest miracle the the world has seen since the resurrection of Yeshua. The Lord even used the secular United Nations organisation to partition Palestine as He worked out His plans.

Then on May 14th 1948 the miracle happened . The nation of Israel dramatically reappeared on the world scene in an amazing fulfilment of the following verses.

Ezekiel 36:8 *"But you, O mountains of Israel, you shall shoot forth your branches and yield your fruit to My people Israel, for they are about to come.*

Isaiah 66:8 *Who has heard such a thing? Who has seen such things? Shall the earth be made to give birth in one day? Or shall a nation be born at once? For as soon as Zion was in labour, she gave birth to her children.*

1967   The Re-unification of Jerusalem

The next major station on the track, and indeed another miracle, was the re-unification of Jerusalem after the Six Day War of 1967. Not only did the Israeli army defeat three neighbouring armies (Egyptian, Jordanian and Syrian), the city of Jerusalem was reunited in Jewish hands for the first time in 1900 years.

This dramatic event inspired many Jews and Christians to take a serious look at Bible prophecy. Thousands of Jews, primarily younger American Jews who were caught up in the Hippie movement of the late 1960's, came to faith in Yeshua as their Messiah.

Very quickly as they began to read the Bible, they realised that from Genesis to Revelation, it is a Jewish book. Many of them realised that they had not been converted to another religion, but they had been 'reverted' to the true faith of Abraham. They were still Jewish, even more so!

A SLOW COMING

The Jewish believers began to form themselves into small Messianic Jewish congregations, where they could worship the God of Israel and Yeshua, the King of the Jews, in a more Jewish style than was available in most churches.

As the numbers of these Messianic congregations began to increase, organizations were raised up to oversee them..

This was primarily taking place in the USA, but soon Jews in many other countries also began to come to faith, and Messianic congregations sprang up all over the world. This phenomenon is known as the 'Modern Messianic Jewish Movement'.

Today, most of the leadership of the Messianic Movement around the world, and even in Israel, are the same Jews who came to faith in the late 1960's and early 1970's, ostensibly as a result of the re-unification of Jerusalem.

1997 Modern Messianic Movement 30 Years Old - Called to the Nations

I originally placed the year 1997 on the map for personal reasons, as that was the year I sensed the Lord impart the vision for **Out of Zion** Ministries. However I now believe that 1997 was a key year for the whole Messianic Jewish Movement.

As I was sharing with a Lydia prayer group in West London in 1998, I felt the Holy Spirit show me the key as to why I had been sensing since the year before, that if it was never time before for Messianic Jews to rise up and fulfil the ancient call to be a blessing and a light to the nations, it was now.

As I was explaining to the Lydia ladies, that I saw 1967 as the birth point of the modern Messianic Movement, I sensed the Holy Spirit remind me that it was during 1997 that the Lord called me to establish **Out of Zion** Ministries. Then I heard these words – "30 years". Suddenly I saw it. Joseph was 30 years old when he moved into his ministry in Egypt. Yeshua was 30 years old when He moved into His 3 year ministry. And I later discovered that 30 was the age of Levitical priesthood. (Numbers 4:23)

Not only was it prophesied that the Jews would return to their land, and not only was it prophesied that they would return to their God and serve the Messiah, but it was prophesied that one day they would indeed be a blessing and a light to the nations. As the Holy Spirit showed me these things at that Lydia meeting, I sensed that the Lord was saying, "the modern Messianic Movement has now come of priestly age – it is time to rise up and fulfil the destiny and calling that I have placed upon my chosen people. "

??? The Last Station - The 2nd Coming of Messiah

Unless there is another station that I am not aware of there now is only one station left. The last station represents the time of the Lord's return. I don't have any idea in which year that will occur. All I know is that it is very, very close.

****

Chapter 2

3500 Years of Anti-Semitism

If we study the history of Israel, we will see that every major move of God has been pre-empted by Satan. The Devil obviously has had prior knowledge of what God is planning to do, and he has tried (unsuccessfully) to prevent the prophecies from coming to pass. Since the days of Adam's and Eve's fall from grace, the Lord has been working out His eternal plan to redeem mankind and reconcile sinful man to Himself. Throughout the last 6000 years, the Devil also had a plan. A plan to deceive mankind, and he has always had a vessel prepared to attempt to thwart the plans of God.

Egypt and the Pharaoh

God destined Israel to be a kingdom of priests, a holy nation (Exodus 19:6). Their task was to carry out His plan of redemption plan to a world now separated from Him by sin. He planned to bring the Hebrew slaves out of Egypt (according to His promise to Abraham), and into the promised land where He would deliver to them (and the world) the Ten Commandments.

A SLOW  COMING

Satan obviously also knew the plan and chose Pharaoh as his vessel to thwart God's plan. He did his best, but was no match for God's appointed deliverer, a man called Moses.

Esther and Haman

We read the account of the next major attempt to destroy the Jewish people in the book of Esther. This event, remembered in the Jewish festival known as Purim, takes place in ancient Persia (Iran). Another evil man, Haman, was impelled by the Devil to put an end to the Jewish people. If it had not been for a wise Jewish man, Mordecai, and another deliverer appointed by God, Esther, a beautiful young Jewess who had found favour in the king's eyes, Haman's attempt to deceive the king into annihilating all of the Jews may have succeeded. Israel and subsequently the Church would not be here today.

Antiochus Epiphanes

In the 2nd century BC, Greek-Syrian General Antiochus ruthlessly ruled over Israel. His demonically inspired attempt to abort the prophetic plan of God for Israel included banning the keeping of the Sabbath and the Holy festivals, outlawing circumcision, and ultimately the desecration of the Temple by sacrificing a pig on the altar.

The Macabee brothers were to be Israel's deliverer on this occasion. In 176 BC Judas Macabee and his brothers revolted against Antiochus, who had by now set himself up as Epiphanes (God manifest). As in the story of David and Goliath, with the Lord's supernatural assistance, this small band of

Jewish zealots overcame the might of the Greco-Syrian empire and Israel lived on.

King Herod

One hundred and seventy years later, as God prepared to introduce His ultimate redemptive masterpiece, His own Son, Yeshua, the Lamb of God, Satan again foreknew the plan, and had another wicked vessel prepared to intervene. What else could have inspired King Herod to murder all the two year old boys at Bethlehem? Satan knew the Messiah had been born and he was desperate to prevent Yeshua from carrying out God's plan of redemption.

Satan's Greatest Mistake - the Cross

Satan failed to kill the infant who was destined to become the Messiah and 30 years later Yeshua commenced His earthly ministry. Satan used yet another wicked man, Judas Iscariot, (in cahoots with the Sanhedrin, and the Romans and Pontius Pilate) to put an end to the earthly work of the Saviour. The Lamb of God was sacrificed on a cross on Jerusalem's Calvary hill, to be resurrected three days later. Satan was now defeated once and for all.

Church Anti-Semitism - Replacement theology

The first 70 years of church history was glorious. The Church grew rapidly and moved in the power of the Holy Spirit. According to Acts chapter 5, signs wonders and miracles were a daily part of the life of the first generation believers.

41

A SLOW COMING

It has been estimated that by the end of the first century, there were approximately one million Jews in Israel who were followers of Yeshua. However circumstances changed dramatically and rapidly. Soon the leadership of the Church was in the hands of non-Jews who seriously misunderstood God's Word in respect to their relationship to Israel and the Jewish people.

Instead of seeing themselves as having been grafted into the nation of Israel as described in Romans 11:17, they were deceived by the devil to believe, and to teach, that God had absolutely finished with the Jewish people, and that the Church was now the Israel of God. As we will see in the chapter on replacement theology, this was not what the Bible said and not what Paul taught. This doctrine from Hell inspired and supported 1900 years of Christian anti-Semitism instead of Christian Zionism, and ultimately led to the darkest deed in man's tenure on the Earth.

Hitler and the Holocaust

Nearly 2000 years later, Satan must have known about the imminent rebirth of the nation of Israel. He found yet another suitable vessel to carry out his evil deeds. Hell must have been very busy as the young Adolf Hitler grew up, seeing to it that he suffered deep rejection. Then spending much of his youth living with an uncle who owned an occult bookshop, the young Adolf Hitler was a prime candidate to be used by the Devil in a yet another attempt to annihilate the Jewish people, and put a stop to the main event of God's end-time plan – the second coming of the Messiah.

Hitler failed and the nation of Israel rose from virtual death and miraculously reappeared on the world scene on May14th 1948. The prophetic clock, stalled since AD 70, began ticking on its final countdown to the now imminent return of the Messiah.

Finally the Anti-Christ

I believe that as we approach the "*great and awesome Day of the Lord*" (Joel 2:31) we will see Hell's final attempt by Satan to destroy Israel. This time it will be Satan's masterpiece – the Anti-Christ! It is his last chance to stop the prophesied word of God, the kingdom of God finally being established upon the earth, from coming to pass. Satan knows that this will bring about his total and eternal defeat. However we have the luxury of being able to read the actual end of the story in the last chapters of the book of Revelation.

The good news is **God wins !!!** The prophecies are all fulfilled, allowing Heaven to release Yeshua (Acts 3:21) so that He may return as the Lion of the Tribe of Judah, to take up His royal throne in the Temple in Jerusalem. And the Devil and his followers are consigned to the pit for the 1000 years.

If you are a follower of Yeshua, then you are on the winning side!

****

Chapter 3

The Mystery of the Olive Tree

In Romans chapter 9, 10 and especially 11, the Lord brings revelation through the Apostle Paul, making it obligatory for the Church to understand her relationship with Israel.

Let us see how the Word of God describes the relationship of the Church with Israel. He warns the grafted-in branches (Gentile Christians) not to be arrogant against the natural branches (the Jews) as it is the Jewish roots that support them. If God cut the Jews off, He can cut the Gentiles off too.

Romans 11:18 *do not boast against the branches. But if you do boast, remember that you do not support the root, but the root supports you.*

When we study and understand Church history, we see that the Devil deceived the early Church into adopting a Greek or Hellenistic form of Christianity, instead of being adopted into the Hebraic roots of the true faith as taught by Yeshua Himself to the first Messianic believers.

A SLOW COMING

In Romans 11 Paul calls this a *mystery*. There are several other places in the Bible that also speak of mysteries, and I think that if the Bible calls something a mystery, we need to make a point to understand what the mystery is. So I want to talk about the mystery in Romans 11.

Romans 11:25 *For I do not desire, brethren, that you should be ignorant of this mystery, lest you should be wise in your own opinion, that blindness in part has happened to Israel until the fullness of the Gentiles has come in.*

Lets go back to the beginning of the chapter.......
Romans 11:1 *I say then, Has God cast away his people?*

The answer to the question is **GOD FORBID,** some translations say **CERTAINLY NOT**. To my understanding either rendition is a very strong Biblical statement that the replacement doctrine is not scriptural, to say the very least! Lets read on ....

Romans 11:11 *I say then, have they stumbled that they should fall? Certainly not! But through their fall, to provoke them to jealousy, salvation has come to the Gentiles.*

I understand this to mean that the majority of Jewish people have fallen temporarily from God's grace, and the Gospel of salvation has come to the Gentiles instead, in order for them to provoke the Jews to jealousy. Right here we see that God's plan was always for the Gentiles to bring the Jewish people to a knowledge of their Messiah.

Romans 11:17 *And if some of the branches were broken off, and you, being a wild olive tree, were grafted in among them, and with them became a partaker of the root and fatness of the olive tree .....*

46

In scripture Israel is often referred to as an 'Olive Tree'. Picture an olive tree - it has roots, a trunk and branches. The roots of the natural olive tree are anointed roots, and we can only be connected to these anointed roots if we are grafted into the natural Olive Tree - Israel.

These roots lead back to the patriarchs, to Abraham, Isaac and Jacob. The natural branches are the people who by birth are the seed of Abraham, the physical descendants of the twelve tribes of Israel. When we are grafted into this natural tree, we become partakers of the fatness of the olive tree and to continue to draw from the nutrition of this tree, we have to remain in its roots.

The Bible describes the Gentiles as being cut out of a wild olive tree, cut out of other cultures and religious traditions, and grafted into the natural olive tree of Israel. The analogy of being 'grafted-in' shows the intimacy that God intended Gentile believers to have with the Jewish people.

This is how God sees the Gentile body of Messiah in relationship to the Jewish people. She is 'grafted-in' and now shares in the anointing of the natural roots. We must see things as God sees them and not create our own doctrines or theology - not to be 'wise in our own opinion'.

The NIV translation gives an even stronger image. It says that from the roots of the natural tree comes 'nourishing sap'. When the Church fathers fell for this Satanic lie and began to see themselves as having replaced the natural olive tree, they effectively cut themselves off from the fatness, the nourishing sap that only comes from the Jewish roots.

A SLOW COMING

Signs, wonders and miracles were a normal part of the daily lives of the 1st century Church. The supernatural gifts of the Holy Spirit were strongly in evidence during this period. However church history books record that at the same time as this replacement teaching entered the Church, the 'dunimos' power of the Holy Spirit departed. The signs and wonders decreased. The miracles decreased and the Baptism of the Holy Spirit and the Five Fold Ministry gifts were also lost to the majority of the Church.

The Church began to walk the path that took her into a period known as the 'Dark Ages'. If you have every studied the Dark Ages, you probably cringed as I did, when I learned of just some of the horrors committed by people calling themselves "Christians". This was indeed a time of darkness and it lasted of 1,000 years. The Bible tells us that *God is Light and in Him there is no darkness.* How then, did the Church of the Living God, supposedly filled with, and being led by His Holy Spirit, find herself 'powerless', in a 1000 year vacuum of darkness?

It is my opinion that the answer to this question is that this darkness came over the Church as the majority of leaders embraced 'Replacement' theology, causing her to be cut off and removed from the source of the power (the nourishing sap), and from the source of the 'Light'.

In the section entitled "The Restoration of the Church", we will see that there has been a parallel restoration taking place, alongside the restoration of Israel. As the Lord has been restoring Israel, He has also been restoring the Church, as He prepares to reconnect both the natural and the wild branches to the Biblical roots of the Olive Tree.

The final part of the restoration of Israel is to be restored to her apostolic calling, and the last element that is now beginning to be restored to the Church, is the restoration to her Biblical roots.

I concur with fellow 'Kiwi', and prophetic evangelist, Peter Robertson, who wrote the following in an article entitled "The Olive Tree" : *It is no coincidence that when the Church legislated her own "divorce" from Judaism around the 4th century, the Holy Spirit and His gifts began their gradual disappearance. Nor is it a further coincidence that in the 20th century, restoration of the Holy Spirit to the Church has been perfectly synchronized with, and in fact has been a consequence of the restoration of Israel ......*

We are still working through what it means to be restored to the Jewish roots, or as I prefer to call them, the Biblical roots. If we take it one step at a time and stay open to the leading of the Holy Spirit, He will surely show us the way to go. An excellent start is to begin to study and celebrate the Biblical Feasts. These are not Jewish feasts; God calls them His feasts (Leviticus 23:2) and from them we can glean treasures of who our God and Messiah really is. The Biblical feast can also help us know where we are, in prophetic time, as the feast cycle is a 'calendar' of the Lords plan of redemption for all of mankind.

No wonder the Lord calls it a mystery and Paul writes very emphatically, that we ought not be ignorant of the **Mystery of the Olive Tree.**

Romans 11:25 *For I do not desire, brethren, that you should be ignorant of this mystery ....*

A SLOW COMING

If you are still ignorant of this mystery, and this book has whetted your appetite, may I suggest you repent for being ignorant all these years, and having received forgiveness, pray and ask the Holy Spirit to be your teacher. There are also many good books available to help you in your search.

****

Chapter 4

The Historical Reality

Romans 11:25 *For I do not desire, brethren, that you should be ignorant of this mystery, lest you should be wise in your own opinion ...*

The subject of Israel and the Jewish people has been a point of contention in the church for nearly 2000 years now. Many have been taught and believed that the Church replaced Israel as "the apple of God's eye" and that His covenant promises were taken from the Jewish people and given to the believing church exclusively. However, there has always been a remnant who saw the truth of the matter according to God's Word, and who In the face of much opposition and even persecution, stood with and for Israel and the Jewish people.

In his book 'The Harvest' Rick Joyner shares a prophetic vision of end-time events that he was given in 1987.(see Introduction) As an evangelist, I too am very concerned that many good people, who have gone to church all of their lives, will make a mistake of eternal proportions as they follow the anti-Christ into the false end-time church, a church that will follow in the

A SLOW  COMING

footsteps of the apostate church of the last 1900 years, which has despised and persecuted Israel and the Jewish people.

The First 100 Years

It was not until Paul's time that God revealed to the apostles that Peter was to take the Gospel to the Jews and Paul was to be the apostle to the Gentiles. So we see that the early Church consisted of mainly Jewish people who had accepted that Yeshua was indeed the Messiah who had been prophesied of in our Holy Scriptures, the Old Testament. They carried on their life, observing Jewish traditions, but found greatly increased fulfilment through the knowledge and relationship with their Messiah. By the end of the first century there were an estimated 1,000,000 Jewish believers in Israel, and through Jewish apostles, the gospel rapidly spread through the Middle East and Europe towards Rome.

The Schism - Replacement Theology

After many years of cruel persecution against Christianity the Roman emperor Constantine made it the official Roman religion in A.D. 325. Prior to this, there was the universal (catholic) church and the Roman Empire, but subsequently the Roman Catholic Church and the "Holy" Roman Empire! Even the structure of the church hierarchy took on the form of the Roman military order.

As this new Romanised form of Christianity found its way back to Israel, and out to the other nations, it carried with it many of the pagan attributes of Rome. These pagan practices were offensive and unacceptable to the Jewish believers who knew the truth of God's scriptures. These early Messianic Jews now found themselves not only persecuted by unbelieving Jews, but also by the church because they refused to adopt these new ways and soon their numbers began to significantly decrease.

Replacement Theology

The Devil knows what is written in the Bible, and he has had a plan to abort the plans and purposes of God. He tried to prevent Yeshua's first coming, and he has a plan to prevent His second coming, thus extending his lordship of the Earth. How? By deceiving the people of God with a doctrine that comes straight from the pit of hell, the doctrine known as Replacement Theology.

Many of the Church fathers were deceived by this false doctrine, and if we again look at church history, we see the power of God, that we read about in the book of Acts left the Church at the same time replacement theology took hold. They cut themselves off from the source of the power of God, the Biblical roots of the Christian faith.

Derek Prince states in his book 'Who Owns the Land': *There has been a tremendous amount of misunderstanding amongst sincere Christians concerning God's dealing with Israel. I don't believe that this misunderstanding is entirely natural. I think there is a spiritual force behind it. Satan has been very busy keeping Christians in ignorance of the Lord's plans and purposes for Israel, because we all have a part to play in God's plans. Consequently Satan resists our coming into an understanding and thus becoming qualified to play our part in what God is doing.*

A SLOW 🚂 *COMING*

Derek goes on to say, *We owe our entire spiritual inheritance to Israel. If there had been no Israel there would have been no patriarchs, no prophets, no apostles, no Bible, and most of all no Saviour. We are all debtors to the Jewish people.* (end quote)

Yeshua said that He came to take down the middle wall of partition between Jew and Gentile. When Replacement Theology took root the wall was rebuilt, but this time it was everything Jewish that was thrown out. The Shabbat, the Holy Festivals of God and many other things were lost to the Body of Messiah. The situation went steadily downhill and led the Church into the Dark Ages, from which we are yet to fully emerge.

Today as we stand on the brink of the "Great Tribulation" that precedes the return of Yeshua, I believe that the truth concerning Israel is the final, and perhaps the most important revelation which God is restoring to the Church since the reformation. I pray that as you read on, you will gain a true perspective of the relationship between Israel and the Church of Yeshua the Messiah, King of the Jews.

See Appendix 2 on page 176 for a comprehensive explanation of Replacement Theology

Lies and Persecution

The Jewish people and Christians are all sons and daughters under the same Father, the God of Israel, but their treatment at the hands of many who claimed to be Christians has been atrocious. If we take a look at some of the events of the last

2000 years, I am sure that the following details of Church-inspired lies and persecution directed against the Jews will astound and shock you....

• From the early church onward preachers have claimed that Jews were cursed by God, abandoned by Him, and were sons of the devil

• Eusebius claimed that Christianity predated Judaism, and that the prophets and other saints were in fact Christians.

• In the 2nd century Marcian claimed that the God of the Old Testament was a different God to the Christian God, and therefore the Old Testament should be discarded as scripture.

• St. Augustine preached "O Church of God, thy enemy is the heathen the Jew......"

• John Chrysostom, Patriarch of Constantinople (A.D. 344-407), an early leader of the church, stated: "Jews are the most worthless of men - they are lecherous, greedy, rapacious...they worship the devil. It is incumbent on all Christians to hate Jews". He also claimed that Jews don't worship God in their synagogues, but sacrifice their sons and daughters to devils, describing synagogues as the devil's refuge – Satan's synagogue.

• Throughout the crusades Jews who were unwilling to submit to baptism were put to death. Many Jewish people were burned, beaten, and crucified on a cross as on-lookers yelled "Christ killers!" In AD 1099, crusaders in Jerusalem burnt the temple to the ground with the Jews of the city inside. While the temple burned, the crusaders "marched around the synagogue chanting ' Christ we adore thee'

A SLOW  COMING

- At the coronation of Richard the Lionhearted in 1190 the Jews were proclaimed in the liturgy as sons of the devil over whom the Church triumphs.

- In 1290 all Jews were expelled from England

- St. Bernard of Clareveaux, the greatest preacher of 12th century Europe declared "The bestial Jews are lower than the animals and descendants of the devil.."

- In 1343 in Germershein, Germany after local Jews were accused of a ritual murder, the entire Jewish community was burned at the stake.

- In Prague in 1390 a few Jewish children threw sand at a Catholic priest.-3000 Jews were massacred as punishment.

- A leading Jewish historian, Cecil Rote believed that as many as half of the Jews in Europe during the Middle Ages, died violent deaths at the hands of Christians. For a small Jewish wrong, the Christians would repay a hundredfold. When one Jew was falsely accused of murdering a Christian child an entire Jewish community could be burnt at the stake

- In the 15th century the Catholic Church was responsible for the Spanish Inquisition and ultimately the expulsion of all the Jews from Spain in 1492

- The most famous preacher of the 15th century, St. Vincent Ferra personally organized the creation of the Spanish ghettos and the passing of anti-Jewish laws. He said, "Christians must not kill Jews with knives but with words."

• It has often been claimed by Christians that Jews kidnapped Christian children to use for sacrifices in the synaguguo on Holy Festivals.

• 'Christians' also claimed that the Jews were responsible for the Black Death that killed millions in Europe because they didn't suffer from it. It was the Jews' observance of Gods laws of personal hygiene and the food laws that saved them from plague and disease.

• Martin Luther, the father and noted hero of the Protestant Reformation, at first claimed the Jewish people to be "in-laws, blood related, and cousins". But when they did not join Luther in his assault on the Roman Church, Luther said: "All the Blood kindred of Christ burn in Hell, and they are rightly served, even according to their own words they spoke to Pilate".

• Luther printed up vicious and hateful statements. In his tract "On the Jews and Their Lies" Luther asserts "Know this, Christian, you have no greater enemy than the Jew". Luther also entreated action against the Jewish people: He demanded that their synagogues be burned to the ground, their books destroyed, their homes laid waste.

• In the late 1800's 'Christians' were responsible for the circulation of "The Protocols of the Elders of Zion", a forgery which propagated a Jewish conspiracy to take over the world These papers caused much anti-Semitism and persecution in the 20th century, and are still being touted by Arab nations today.

• Hitler loved Luther's teachings. Luther was a prominent authority advocating some of the very same principles that 400 years later were a key part of Hitler's ideology. Luther and others

helped give Hitler the necessary endorsement to set in motion the mass genocide of millions of Jews

• In 1933 the Nazis declared that all Jews had to wear a star. One month later convoys began to take them away to the death camps. Church leaders and Christianity in general did very little to save the Jewish people. Fortunately there were some exceptions and beloved saints such as Corrie Ten Boom helped to save the lives of many Jews.

• Hitler was held in high regard by many leaders of the German Church, being venerated and almost worshiped by the people. Many 'Christians' assisted in the massacre of Jews. Two thirds of the S.S. were baptised members of churches. Six million Jews and millions of others (many of whom were Christians) perished at the hands of the Nazis.

The Greatest Lie of All

From the days of the early church and onward, preachers have claimed that Jews were cursed by God, abandoned by Him, and were sons of the Devil. Consequently, the evolving church was now almost illiterate with regards to Jewish customs and culture. New Christians were educated with false interpretations, which allowed anti-Semitism to flourish.

Perhaps the greatest lie perpetuated by the Church has been the denial of the Jewishness of Yeshua. Even today most Christians don't comprehend Yeshua as an observant Torah loving Jew. In virtually all church art Yeshua has been depicted as Gentile. Instead of perceiving Him as the God of Israel and the Jews, the Church has made God in its image, be it Latin,

Anglo-Saxon or taken to today's extremes, black or feminine. These humanistically conceived gods and messiahs reflect man's pride and ambition to be in absolute control of his own destiny.

Since much of the Church denied the fact that Gentile Christians were called to join with Israel in covenant with the God of the Bible, the Church adopted a form of natural religion with its own saints and idols. Historians have shown clear parallels between worship of the Virgin Mary, often called the Mother of God, to the 'Great Mother' goddess religions. The Church abandoned the biblical Festivals and replaced them with the fertility festivals of mid-winter (December) and Easter, thinly disguised by relating them to events in the life and times of Yeshua. Jewish believers were forced to renounce their Jewishness and abandon their observance of God's Festivals, which are a prophetic outline of Gods redemption plan and end-time calendar.

The Church has largely behaved like Cain towards Abel and Jacob to Esau, and has taken its elder brother's birthright, claiming that it has replaced its brother in God's affection. We must recognise that church leaders in every generation have denied that Christians are brothers with the Jews, worshiping the same Father. A large proportion of Christian teaching has been based on Replacement Theology.

Is it any wonder the Jewish people have such a distrust and of Christians and hatred of the Jesus in whose name these things were carried out. The Church of today needs to repent of its past attitude and behaviour towards the Jews and begin to reach out to the Jewish people in brotherly love and with a genuine heart felt concern for their salvation.

A SLOW COMING

The result of the Church's falling into the trap of following the dictates of Satan is evident in the following two quotations. These quotes are from Jews, the very people whom the Christian Church was called to provoke to jealousy. The following quotes are taken from Dr Michael Brown's book 'Our Hands Are Stained With Blood': (page 90 / 91)

1/ Professor Eugene Borowitz: *We might be more inclined to give some Christian claims credence, had we seen Christians through the ages behave as models of redeemed humanity. Looking through the window of history we have found them in as much need of saving as the rest of humankind. If anything, their social failings are especially discrediting of their doctrine for they claim to be uniquely free of human sinfulness and freshly inspired by their faith to bring the world to a realm of love and peace. Until sinfulness ceases and well-being prevails, Jews know the Messiah has not come.*

2/ Leading Jewish thinker Eliazer Berkovits: *After 19 centuries of Christianity, the extermination of six million Jews, among them one and a half million children, carried out in cold blood in the very heart of Christian Europe, encouraged by the criminal silence of virtually all Christendom, including that of an infallible Holy Father in Rome, was the natural culmination of this [moral and spiritual] bankruptcy [of the Christian religion]. A straight line runs from the first acts of oppression against the Jews and Judaism in the 4th century to the Holocaust in the 20th.*

These Jewish men may not understand the difference between true and nominal Christianity, but can you not sense the grief and pain that pervades the Jewish heart? Is it any wonder the Jews don't want to hear about Jesus, the 'Christian Messiah'!

The Awakening

I believe that Satan always made a point of blinding many in the church to the truth concerning God's plan for Israel and the Jewish people, so that he could continue with his age-old scheme to destroy the nation God chose to use to bring redemption to the whole world. Satan knew that if he destroyed the olive tree (Israel) then ALL of the branches would die.

But the destiny of the Church was not to remain in darkness. The seeds of God's heart for Israel were already sprouting, even as anti-Semitism continued to be a persistent root in the Church. In the 16th Century Martin Luther obviously had a revelation of the importance of the Jews coming back to faith in their God and Messiah. He set out to reach the Jews with the gospel. Unfortunately when they didn't respond in the manner he expected, he had a change of heart towards the Jewish people, verbally and physically persecuting the Jews. Ultimately his vicious anti-Semitic teachings became responsible for inspiring Adolf Hitler's 'final solution' to once and for all rid the world of the Jews.

In the 17h Century the Puritans, known for their Biblical piety were the fore-runners of today's Christian Zionists. The late 19th century Brethren denomination also had a clear understanding of the Old Testament prophecies. The Brethren taught that Israel must soon reappear on the world stage as a fulfilment of the words of the prophets and as a precursor to the second coming of the Messiah.

Throughout the Church age, there has always been a small number of Jewish Christians and some of them have been very prominent people. Benjamin Disraeli, the British Prime

A SLOW  COMING

Minister was a believer, and many famous Rabbis found the truth of the Messiah and were born again.

Today hundreds of thousands of Jews have again accepted Yeshua as their Messiah. There are many groups such as Jews For Jesus, The Messianic Jewish Alliance of America, Union of Messianic Jewish Congregations, Chosen People Ministries and many more smaller groups.

As of 2002, there are approximately four hundred Messianic fellowships worldwide, and today in Israel there are more than eighty Messianic congregations. We clearly see that in accordance with His Word, God is lifting the veil off His chosen people, in ever-increasing numbers, more evidence of the closeness of the end of this age and the return of Messiah.

****

Chapter 5

Times of Restoration

Acts 3:20-21 ..... *that He may send Jesus Christ, who was preached to you before, "whom heaven must receive until the times of restoration of all things, which God has spoken by the mouth of all His holy prophets since the world began.*

In the above verse, we see that a time of restoration must precede the Lord's return. I believe that we are now living in the time when the Lord is having mercy on, and rebuilding Zion.

Psalm 102:13 *You will arise and have mercy on Zion; for the time to favour her, yes, the set time, has come.*

Ps 102:16 *For the LORD shall build up Zion; he shall appear in His glory.*

As the 20th century dawned, this rebuilding process began and over the last 100 years, we have seen many major developments in both parts of Zion, Israel and the Church.

A SLOW  COMING

Restoration of Israel

In Matthew 16:3, Yeshua speaks about knowing the timing of God. For those who have lived during the last 100 years, it should have been obvious that God is at work fulfilling the prophecies referred to in Acts chapter 3:21. There are hundreds of verses referring to Israel's return at the end of the age - for example

Jeremiah 16:14 *"Behold the days are coming," says the Lord, "that it shall be no more said 'The Lord lives who brought up the children of Israel from the land of Egypt', but 'the Lord lives who brought up the children of Israel from the Land of the North where He had driven them.' For I will bring them back into their land which I gave to their fathers."*

Jeremiah 30:3 *"For behold the days are coming says the Lord that I shall bring back from captivity my people Israel and Judah, says the Lord and I will cause them to return to the land I gave their fathers, and they shall possess it "*

Ezekiel 37:21 *Thus says the Lord God "Surely I will take the children of Israel from among the nations wherever they have gone, and will gather them from every side and bring them into their own land."*

Isaiah 43:5 *"Fear not for I am with you, I will bring your descendants from the east and gather you from the west, I will say to the north "Give them up" and to the south "do not keep them back … bring my sons from afar and my daughters from the ends of the earth."*

The Lord arose and began to have mercy on Zion as He initiated the "times of restoration" in 1897, the year of the first Zionist Congress in Basel, Switzerland.

Then on May 14th 1948 the restoration process accelerated. The nation of Israel was reborn in one day, just as had been prophesied.

Ezekiel 37:8 *O mountains of Israel, shoot forth your branches for my people Israel are about to come.*

Isaiah 66:8 *Can a nation be born in one day; whoever heard of such a thing?*

Already the "dry bones" of Ezekiel 37:4 were rattling as the Lord began to restore the 'sinow, the flesh and the skin' of the Jewish people and they began to rise up to become part of the great army of five million plus Jews who have returned to Israel in the last 100 years. Now it was time for the Jewish people to have the 'Ruach', the breath restored.

Ezekiel 37:9 *Prophesy to the breath, prophesy son of man and say to the breath, "Thus says the Lord God – Come from the four winds O breath and breathe on these slain that they may live."*

The Biblical Hebrew word for breath is the same word for Spirit. Today in Israel and all over the world there many Jews who have had the Ruach ha Kodesh, the Holy Spirit, breathed into them as they have accepted Yeshua as their personal Messiah. This is also seen in many other verses.

Hosea 3:5 *Afterward the children of Israel shall return and seek the Lord their God and David their King.*

King David had been dead for hundreds of years when Hosea and Jeremiah wrote that. "David your King " refers to the Messiah.

A SLOW  COMING

This return to faith began in earnest as Jerusalem was reunited in 1967. The following statistics give a very good picture of the progress of the Lord's restoration process.

The Growth of the Messianic Movement

	1967	2000
Messianic Fellowships in Israel	very few	90
Messianic Fellowships Worldwide	very few	400
Estimated # Messianic Jews in Israel	50	5000
Estimated # Messianic Jews Worldwide	???	500,000

These statistics represent a modern miracle. It is a major part of God's plan leading up to the second coming of the Messiah. Therefore why is it that very few pastors teach their congregations about God's plan for Israel?   Most church leaders totally ignore what has been happening and is happening in Israel.

I believe that the return of the Jewish people to their homeland is a significant sign pointing to the end of this age and the soon return of the Messiah to Jerusalem. According to Acts 3:21 the Lord is not coming until these prophecies are completely fulfilled. This should be 'big news' to all those who are eagerly awaiting His return.

Psalm 102:13 *You will arise and have mercy on Zion; for the time to favour her, yes, the set time, has come.*
v 14   *For Your servants take pleasure in her stones, and*
       show favour to her dust.

v 15   *So the nations shall fear the name of the LORD, and*
  all the kings of the earth   Your glory.
v 16   *For the LORD shall build up Zion; He shall appear in*
  His glory.

It is obvious, or should be obvious from the word of God that the restoration of Israel is a pre-requisite and a precursor to the Lord's return.

Psalm 102:16   *For the Lord will build up Zion - (then) He will appear in His Glory.*

In fact one of the reasons that the Lord is doing this, is to get the attention of the world, so that they may know He is God.

Isaiah 11:11   *It shall come to pass in that day that the Lord shall set His hand again for a second time to recover the remnant of His people who are left.*

Isaiah 11:12   *He will set up a banner for the nations and will assemble the outcasts of Israel and will gather together the dispersed of Judah from the four corners of the earth.*

This must come as a shock to Christians who have been led to believe that the Lord is coming back for a bride that does not include Israel.

****

A SLOW  COMING

Restoration of the Church
(First the Natural then the Spiritual (1 Corinthians 15:46)

When the Bible talks about 'Zion', it means Israel. However if the Church is truly grafted in to the natural roots, she is also 'Zion'. The Lord began the restoration process with the natural part of Zion, then moved to begin the restoration of the grafted in part of Zion.

Almost as if 'someone' had flicked a switch as the 20th century dawned, there was a mighty outpouring of the Holy Spirit and a renewal of the spiritual gifts in a small Bible school at Topeka, Kansas, led by Charles Parham who had been teaching his students about holiness and righteousness. Soon followed the Welsh revival in 1904 and the Azusa St. revival in 1906. These events brought about the restoration of lost doctrines of early Christianity, tongues, healing and deliverance and the Pentecostal and Charismatic revivals followed. I believe we are presently seeing a revival of the Prophetic and Apostolic ministries.

The final part of the Church's restoration will be the restoration to her biblical roots and centre on her relationship to Israel.

Perhaps you can recall the uproar and controversy that rocked and split many churches, when God brought back the gifts of tongues, healing, and deliverance. Many said 'it is of the devil'. As I have already shown in the introduction, God has revealed through the vision given to Rick Joyner that we need to be prepared for an even greater furore over Israel.

Many others in respected ministries are also becoming aware of the truth. Sadly many Christians, because of ignorance or pride, will be left behind as many churches were left behind, powerless and dying, because they refused to follow the leading of the Holy Spirit. So let us not make the same mistake - let us be open to find the truth of what God is doing and what He is saying about His chosen land Israel, and His chosen people the Jews, to the Church today.

The majority of the natural branches, the Jewish people, have fallen from the tree. What happens when a branch falls from a tree, it dies. And now Gentiles, being the wild branches, have been grafted into the tree. But the end of the verse tells us the Jewish branches **WILL** be grafted back in.

Romans 11:24 *For if you were cut out of the olive tree which is wild by nature, and were grafted contrary to nature into a cultivated olive tree, how much more will these, who are natural branches, be grafted into their own olive tree?*

****

A SLOW  COMING

The Relevance of the Restoration of Israel

By this stage of our journey, it should have become strikingly clear, what the relevance of God's dealings with Israel is. As we have travelled down the 'Slow Train Coming' map, we have seen that everything God has in mind has centred around Israel and the Jewish people. Israel is the key to the world's redemption and the Devil's destruction.

God has made Israel a 'banner to the nations', a large sign. Israel is the indicator as to where the train is on the track. If you refer back to the map on page 28/29, place your finger where we are in time.

The slow train, which has been coming down the track now for 6000 years, picked up speed in 1897 as the Zionist Congress met. It picked up more speed in 1948 when Israel suddenly reappeared on the world scene. And when Jerusalem was re-united in 1967, the turbo came on!

We are near the end of the journey and the train is now thundering down the track at breakneck speed. Although many Christians have no idea where the train is, the Devil has been watching it very closely.

The restoration of Israel and the Jewish people is like a bright signal lamp beaming beside the track. It is beaming towards the Jewish people saying "you can believe in Yeshua and still be Jewish". It is beaming towards the Christians saying "look where the train is. Time is very short. Get on with the work of the Kingdom". And it is beaming into the eyes of the Devil saying, "Devil, your time is nearly up ".

The Devil has known where the train has been throughout history, and he has continually tried to throw a spanner on the track, attempting to derail the train.

I believe all Hell shook on May 14th 1948, because when Israel was restored as a nation, the Devil knew it was a sign that the Lord was coming soon. I also think Hell shook again in 1967, because when Jerusalem was reunited, the Devil knew that it was a sign that the Lord's return was even sooner. And I wouldn't be surprised if Hell shakes every Friday night and Saturday morning.

Why do I think that? Well, allow me to be very Jewish and answer a question with a question. Keeping in mind Acts 3:21, that Heaven is holding back the Lord's return until the all of the words of the prophets are fulfilled, who was the greatest of all the prophets? The answer is Yeshua. What did He say?

In Matthew 23:39 Yeshua prophesied to a group of Jews in Jerusalem, "*You won't see me again until you say Baruch Ha Bah B'Shem Adonai (Blessed is he who comes in the name of the Lord).*" These words, coming out of Jewish lips, are the key that unlocks the gates of Heaven, allowing the Lord to return.

The reason why I think Hell shakes every Friday night and Saturday morning is that this is when the 400 plus Messianic congregations around the world have their Sabbath meetings. And most of us sing that song, "Baruch Ha Bah".

Not all of us sing it at the same time, but enough of us that it is heard in Hell and the Devil is extremely nervous, because he knows the relevance of Messianic Jews singing those words indicates that – his time is short.

A SLOW COMING

Israel's restoration as a world nation in 1948 was a sign of the closeness of the 2nd coming of Messiah. And the restoration of the Messianic Jewish believers since 1967 is a similar sign. We are currently just a 'saved remnant', but we are the first-fruit evidence that *'All Israel is about to be saved'* (Romans 11:26), and that means, as the song says, that "soon and very soon we are going to see the King".....

This song is talking about King Yeshua, sitting on the throne of David, in the Temple in Jerusalem.

****

Chapter 6

One New Man

Eph 2:15 *For He Himself is our peace, who has made both one, and has broken down the middle wall of separation, having abolished in His flesh the enmity, that is the law of commandments contained in ordinances, creating* **ONE NEW MAN** *from two, thus making peace.*

Because the above verse has been the cause of much misunderstanding and controversy in the Body of Messiah, I want to take a closer look at the meaning of that term.

What is a One New Man Congregation?

A One New Man congregation is a church, congregation or fellowship where 'born-again' Jews and born-again Gentiles worship and serve the God of Israel and His Son, Yeshua the Messiah in a Biblically based setting.

A SLOW  COMING

Who Attends a One New Man Congregation?

There are various terms commonly used to describe followers of Yeshua – Christians, Believers, Messianic Jews, Jewish Christians, Jewish Believers and Hebrew Christians.

A Jew who comes to faith in the Jewish Messiah is still Jewish, even more so. A Gentile who comes to faith in the Jewish Messiah is still a Gentile. According to the Bible, there are only two types of people in the World – Jews and Gentiles. Jews are people with a physical connection to Abraham, through Isaac and Jacob, while every other people group who cannot claim that physical heritage are called Gentiles. The word Gentile is not an insult. It comes from the Hebrew word **goyim**, which in English translates as **nations.**

According to Biblical definitions, there are only two types of Believers.

1/ **Messianic Jews**   or   **Jewish Christians**
2/ **Messianic Gentiles**   or   **Christian Gentiles**

Why is it Important?

We are all born either one or the other. Nothing can ever change the fact of who or what we are, and none of us should even desire to be the other. God created us to be just the way He created us male, female, Jew or Gentile. As much as the Lord definitely does not intend for us to change gender, He does not intend for us to change our racial orientation either. And there is a very important reason for this. As we will read in the next chapter, the God of Israel is a God of **covenant, destiny and calling**. Messianic Jews and Gentiles enjoy the same

covenant, and the same destiny. Our calling is the only difference.

We will read in the next chapter that Jews are called to be a
light and a blessing, while Gentiles are called to provoke the
Jewish people to jealousy. We need to maintain our physical
identity, so that we can fulfill our Kingdom calling.

Have You Seen the One New Man?

This is a question that has been posed to me on several occa-
sions. My answer is a very definite yes! In my various travels,
I have had the privilege of worshipping at several Christian
churches in different countries that have caught hold of the
vision of the meaning of One New Man.

What Does the One New Man Look Like?

He looks a little Jewish and a little Christian. He may be
adorned with a Cross and a Star of David together. A One
New Man congregation I once spoke to in Maryland, had a large
cross with a Star of David at its centre and it was draped in a
tallit or Jewish prayer shawl. An Israeli flag is also usually a key
part of the decor.

You may see and hear a Shofar or Rams Horn, and ornate
banners based on Old Testament scriptures adorn the walls
The praise and worship will likely be a mix of Davidic style
songs and more recent songs written by anointed Christian
musicians.

The One New Man may gather together on Saturday or Sunday. The day of worship is not an issue under the New Cov-

enant. Every day is the day to worship the Lord. This has nothing to do with the Lord's Sabbath, which was never changed to Sunday. Sunday may be the 'Lord's Day', but it is not the Sabbath day.

The One New Man congregation will recognize the importance of the Biblical Feasts and will teach, celebrate and enjoy these Holy Days as the yearly calendar follows it's course. Passover, Shavuot, (Pentecost) and Succot (the Feast of Tabernacles) are the most commonly celebrated by the One New Man.

What is a Messianic Congregation?

The term "Messianic Congregation" is in a way, a misnomer. All congregations that believe in Yeshua are in fact 'Messianic', because they believe in the Messiah. However, this term has come to describe congregations that are more Jewish in make-up and expression.

Today there are more than 400 Messianic Congregations worldwide. Unfortunately, because of the way some Messianic congregations have represented themselves, they are seen by a large proportion of the Body of Messiah as being outside of mainstream Christianity, a place mainly for Jewish people and a few Gentiles. However every Messianic congregation I have visited, except in Israel, has had more non-Jews than Jews in its membership.

I see no New Testament basis for separation between Jewish and Gentile believers. Paul and the early apostles did not plant separate Jewish and Gentile congregations. What most people recognize as a Messianic Congregation is actually the closest resemblance of a One New Man congregation. Messianic Jews and Messianic Gentiles, worshiping the God of Israel together in one unified body. An environment where Jews can worship God in a Jewish way and unbelieving Jews can recognize something that is Jewish. But we need to be careful that it does not become too caught up in Judaism, so that an unbelieving Gentile visitor might think he had entered a synagogue by mistake.

****

A SLOW COMING

Chapter 7

Covenant, Destiny and Calling

Covenant

There is only one covenant for salvation. Now, both Jews and Gentiles are subject to the same salvation covenant. Prior to the crucifixion of Yeshua, only the physical seed of Abraham had a covenant with the God of Israel. In fact God made several covenants with the Jewish people. In Genesis chapter 15 God cut a covenant with Abraham. This was an eternal land covenant and still applies today. (See Psalm 105:6–11) The land that God allotted to Abraham's descendants is clearly laid out in Genesis 15:18.

As the Israelites journeyed from Egypt, the Lord made another covenant, with the Jewish people – the Mosaic Covenant. This was a covenant containing ordinances and a sacrificial system to atone for the transgression of God's ordinances.

Only the Jewish people had this relationship with God. The other nations had no hope of salvation. We can see this in Ephesians chapter 2.

A SLOW COMING

Ephesians 2:11-12 *Therefore remember that you, once Gentiles in the flesh— that at that time you were without Christ, being aliens from the commonwealth of Israel and strangers from the covenants of promise, **having no hope** and without God in the world.*

But God had his 'One Track Plan' and that plan included the people of the other nations. Since the time of Jeremiah, the Lord has declared the establishment of another covenant. (see Jeremiah 31:31)

It is also important to know that God seals His covenants by blood. In Genesis 15 we read the gory details of preparing the birds and animals, whose body parts and blood were used to seal the covenant with Abraham.

God also had prepared to seal this New Covenant with blood. This time it was not the blood of a bull or a goat, but the blood of a lamb, a very special Lamb, God's own Son. We read in Revelation 13:8 about the *Lamb Who was slain from the foundation of the world.*

Nearly 2000 years ago, on the cross of Calvary, the Father sacrificed His only begotten Son and the New Covenant was ratified, sealed by the blood of Yeshua. Now the other nations were invited into God's household.

Eph 2:13 *But now in Christ Jesus you who once were far off have been brought near by the blood of Christ.*

The New Covenant brought Jews and Gentiles under the same covenant and into the same olive tree.

Eph 2:19-21 *Now, therefore, you are no longer strangers and foreigners, but fellow citizens with the saints and members of the household of God, having been built on the foundation of the apostles and prophets, Jesus Christ Himself being the chief corner stone, in whom the whole building, being joined together, grows into a holy temple in the Lord ....*

Israel's Destiny and Calling

When we come into covenant with God, we also come into a God-given calling and destiny. He called the natural seed of Abraham, Isaac and Jacob, the Jewish people to be a Royal Priesthood, a Holy Nation, a Blessing and a Light to the Nations. We first read of Israel's calling to be a royal priesthood in the book of Exodus. As God gives His Torah (instructions) to Moses, He also announces this high calling (Ex19:6). However if we go even further back into Israel's chequered history, we see that the calling to be a blessing to the whole world is announced by God at the very inception of the Jewish race. Six times in the book of Genesis, God declares to Abraham that he and his offspring will be a blessing to all the other nations of the world. (Gen 12:3, 18:18, 22:18, 26:4, 27:33, 28:14)

If we consider the natural realm first, we see that throughout history and in our time, many Jewish men and women have indeed fulfilled this scripture and have blessed the world in the spheres of exploration, science, medicine, art, music and government. Jews have been largely responsible for the shaping of the modern world. Although Jews have made up less than one third of one percent of all mankind, over one third of all the people who have impacted life on this planet have been Jewish.

A SLOW COMING

This ratio is totally disproportionate, but it is only because God has elected it to be this way and anointed His chosen people to be a blessing.

Now let us consider the spiritual realm. Unfortunately, speaking as a Jew, I have to acknowledge that we have, as a nation, failed to fulfil the destiny to be a kingdom of priests and a holy nation, and the call to be a blessing and a light to the nations.

Isaiah 49:6 *Indeed He says, 'It is too small a thing that You should be My Servant to raise up the tribes of Jacob, and to restore the preserved ones of Israel; I will also give You as a light to the Gentiles, that You should be My salvation to the ends of the earth."*

The only time we really fulfilled this call was in the first hundred years of the New Testament Church. The apostle Paul and the other apostles and disciples who began to move out from Israel with the Gospel did indeed fulfil the call, but unfortunately history also tells us that this was short-lived.

However, since 1967 we have witnessed the re-establishment of a body of indigenous, Hebrew speaking Jewish believers living, working and worshipping Yeshua in Israel. Now we are seeing a growing number of Israeli believers answering the call to world missions – to take a Biblically Jewish rooted Gospel to the nations. These Jewish apostles may well be the seed of the 144,000 Jewish evangelists of Revelation chapter seven.

The Church's Destiny and Calling

God also has a destiny and special calling upon non-Jews who have joined themselves to Him, through entering into the

New Covenant, cut in the Blood of His Son Yeshua. I believe that my calling as a Messianic Jew, to bless my Gentile brothers and sisters, can be best fulfilled if I help them fulfil their destiny and calling. I take my calling very seriously. I want to hear those words one day *"Well done, true and faithful servant"*.

Do you, my dear brother or sister, want to hear those same words? Yes! – well, if you are not Jewish, then this is what I believe your destiny and calling is ....

Our destiny is the same. We are all called to be a 'royal priesthood – a holy people'. The Jews were given that destiny in Exodus 19:6 and the Church was given the same destiny in 1 Peter 2:9.

Jews and Gentiles enjoy the same covenant and have been given the same destiny. It is our calling that is different. We have already seen that Jews are called to be a blessing and a light.

Gentile Christians are called to be the Lord's fellow workers (1 Corinthians 3:9) and to hasten the day of His coming (2 Peter 3:12). The Word also shows us how we can fulfil that calling by working with Him as He restores the Jewish people to their homeland and to Himself, through faith in His Son Yeshua.

The Bible tells us, *first the natural, then the spiritual.* As Israel was restored as a nation in 1948, the Lord began to call Christians to help Him bring the Jewish people home, physically. Ministries like Ebenezer, Exodus, Exobus, ICEJ, CFI and many others have been responsible for the return of hundreds of thousands of Jewish people to the land of their forefathers.

A SLOW COMING

This is a literal fulfillment of Isaiah 49:22 *Thus says the Lord GOD: "Behold, I will lift My hand in an oath to the nations, and set up My standard for the peoples; they shall bring your sons in their arms, and your daughters shall be carried on their shoulders".*

Then in 1967 the times and seasons of God moved on. Jerusalem was reunited and the Holy Spirit began to move on the hearts of Jewish men and women all over the world.

Now it was time to bring them home spiritually. Again we can see a scriptural calling for the Gentiles to get involved in the salvation of the Jewish people. In Romans 11:11 *"I say then, have they stumbled that they should fall? Certainly not! But through their fall, to provoke them to jealousy, salvation has come to the Gentiles"* and in Isaiah 62:11 *Indeed the LORD has proclaimed to the end of the world: "Say to the daughter of Zion, 'Surely your salvation is coming; behold, His reward is with Him, and His work before Him.'"*

****

In Summation

Messianic Jews

Covenant: The New Covenant sealed by the blood of Yeshua

Destiny: To be a Royal Priesthood - a Holy people

Calling: To be a blessing and a light to the nations

Gentile Christians

Covenant: The New Covenant sealed by the blood of Yeshua

Destiny: To be a Royal Priesthood - a Holy people

Calling: To bring the Jewish people home physically and to bring them home spiritually by provoking them to jealousy.

Brothers and sisters, the express purpose of this book is to inspire and encourage all of us, Jew or Gentile, who have made Yeshua our Lord and Saviour, to rise up and fulfil the awesome destiny and calling into which we have been born-again.

Let's get on with the specific task for which the Lord had called us to His Kingdom at such a time as this, and we will hasten that day that we will stand before the Lord to hear those words, *"Well done, true and faithful servant."*

A SLOW COMING

Part 2

Israel - Present and Future

A SLOW  COMING

Chapter 8

Whose Land Is It Really?

As the day of the Lord's return draws closer we should expect to see an intensifying of the controversy over Israel, and more specifically Jerusalem and the Temple Mount.

This has indeed been the case since the outbreak of Palestinian initiated violence known as the Al Aksa Intifada. However, the root cause of the animosity goes much further back than the visit to the Temple Mount by the Israeli government minister, Ariel Sharon late September 2000.

The current situation was supposed to have been prevented by the Oslo Peace Treaty brokered between the Israelis and the Palestinians in 1993. For several years after the sides began to negotiate, the issue of Jerusalem was set aside, to be dealt with after the other issues had been resolved.

For several years negotiations centred on the general conditions for a broad based Middle East peace treaty. For their part, the Israelis committed to and carried out major withdrawals from much of the territory Israel had occupied since the Six Day War of 1967.

A SLOW COMING

Even in light of the fact that Israel had abided by the Oslo Agreement, the radical Palestinian militia groups continued to attack innocent Israeli citizens. In 1995 and 1996, a series of terrorist bus bombings claimed the lives of dozens of innocent Israeli men, women and children.

A period of relative quiet followed the bus bombings, however many here in Israel were pessimistic of the real motives of the Palestinian leader Yassar Arafat.

Early in 2000 the Oslo negotiations began to focus on the one point that threatened to derail all that had been achieved thus far – Jerusalem. The relations between the two sides began to deteriorate as no compromise could be arrived at. Then in late September Ariel Sharon made his now infamous visit to the Temple Mount.

Even though Sharon had asked for, and received, permission from the PA security chief, Arafat used this visit as a pretext to ignite the Al Aksa Intifada. Sharon received condemnation from around the world, but several in the PA leadership acknowledged that the uprising had been planned for some time before Sharon's visit.

Months earlier, when Israel withdrew from Southern Lebanon, the terror organizations Hizballah, Hamas and Islamic Jihad saw it as a victory. The suggestion was made by Hizballah that the Palestinians should try the same approach of continual violence, to gain a similar victory over the Israelis. Could this have been what inspired Arafat to call for and support the Al Aksa Intifada?

At the time of the completion of this book (May 2002) the Al

Aksa Intifada is in its 20th month. More than 2500 Palestinians have died, the majority of them in the course of attacking Israeli citizens and soldiers. During the same period, more than 450 Israelis have been killed, by far the majority being innocent men, woman and children who were murdered by misguided Palestinians who were under the impression that these despicable acts of terror will secure them a state with Jerusalem as its capital.

These dreadful acts of terror climaxed in March 2002 with one of the lowest acts of terror ever perpetrated against the Jewish people. On the eve of the Passover festival, a demonically inspired Palestinian terrorist exploded himself in a restaurant in Netanya, taking the lives of 27 Jewish people who were guilty of nothing more than celebrating the liberation of their forefathers from the same demon inspired Pharaoh in Egypt 3500 years ago. The fact that they were celebrating the Passover in the very country that God promised to their ancestors, cost them their lives.

The Netanya Passover massacre, as it has come to be known, was the 'straw that broke the camel's back'. The Israeli people and the government of PM Ariel Sharon had been pushed too far. The patience of the Israelis ran out. As we say in the Pesach Seder, "Dayenu!" (Enough!)

During April and May 2002, the Israel Defence Forces were involved in a large scale military offensive code-named "Operation Defensive Shield" against the terrorist network of the world's No 1 arch terrorist, Yassar Arafat. The Middle East and the whole world is on the verge of what could be the regional war that will reveal the man who will sign a seven year peace treaty and start the count-down to the second coming of the Messiah.

A SLOW COMING

As New Covenant members of the household of the God of Israel, and having been called to be His fellow workers we must be sure that we know the truth concerning the situation in the Middle East. The secular media, radio, T.V. and newspapers lie under the control of the Devil. Satan is currently (and temporarily) *the God of this age* (2 Corinthians 4:4) and *the prince of the power of the air* (Ephesians 2:2) and *the whole world lies under his influence*. (1 John 5:19). He is the one *who deceives the whole world*. (Revelation 12:9)

The Biblical Perspective

Christians have no business turning to secular sources for the answer to the question **Whose Land Is It?** The Bible is the only legitimate authority on this matter.

Follow me through the following verses and we will know for sure the answer to that question.

Psalm 24:1 *The Earth is the Lords and all its fullness.*

The world is the Lord's and He can do with it as He pleases

Psalm 115:16 *The Heavens, even the Heavens are the Lords, but the Earth He has given to the children of men*

We have no access to Heaven yet, but He has given us the Earth. Adam was given full dominion over the Earth.

Acts 17:26 *And He has made from one blood every nation of men to dwell on all the face of the earth, and has determined their preappointed times and the boundaries of their dwellings.*

The Lord has pre-appointed when and where we live.

Now for the most legitimate 'land deed' ever written ....

Psalm 105:6-11 *O descendants of Abraham his servant. O sons of Jacob, his chosen ones. He is the LORD our God; his judgments are in all the earth. He remembers his covenant forever, the word he commanded, for a thousand generations, the covenant he made with Abraham, the oath he swore to Isaac. He confirmed it to Jacob as a decree, to Israel as an everlasting covenant: "To you I will give the land of Canaan as the portion you will inherit."*

If you look at an older Bible map and then at a newer map, you will see that the land once called Canaan, is exactly the same land now known as Israel. And you will also see that the above verses that constitute this eternal land deed there is no mention of Ishmael.

The Arab / Jewish conflict which has continually been the cause of untold death and destruction, and now threatens to engulf the entire world, can never be resolved until the Arabs and the rest of the world come to the realisation that the Creator of the universe has decreed that all of Israel and beyond (Genesis 15:18) legitimately belongs to the Jewish descendants of Abraham.

"Yes", some may say, "but Israel broke the covenant." No she didn't. If we look at the story as it unfolds in Genesis 15:12 the Lord put Abraham to sleep. The procedure in cutting a covenant was that the two parties would walk backwards and forwards in the body parts and the blood, speaking out their covenant promises. When God made the Abrahamic covenant, Abraham was asleep, God promised Abraham the land, but Abraham promised nothing. The Jews have no covenant promise to break!

A SLOW  COMING

Israel or Palestine - 20 Interesting Facts

Here is a list of some conveniently overlooked facts in the current Middle East situation.

1. Nationhood and Jerusalem Israel became a nation in 1312 B.C.E., two thousand years before the rise of Islam.

2. Arab refugees in Israel began identifying themselves as part of a Palestinian people in 1967, two decades after the establishment of the modern State of Israel.

3. Since the Jewish conquest in 1272 B.C.E. the Jews have had dominion over the land for 1000 years with a continuous presence in the land for the past 3,300 years.

4. The only Arab dominion since the conquest in 635 C.E. lasted no more than 22 years.

5. For over 3,300 years, Jerusalem has been the Jewish capital. Jerusalem has never been the capital of any Arab or Muslim entity. Even when the Jordanians occupied the city of Jerusalem, they never sought to make it their capital, and Arab leaders did not come to visit.
6. Jerusalem is mentioned over 700 times in the Jewish Scriptures. Jerusalem is not mentioned once in the Koran.

7. King David founded the city of Jerusalem. Mohammed never came to Jerusalem.

8. Jews pray facing Jerusalem. Muslims pray with their backs toward Jerusalem.

9. Arab and Jewish Refugees. In 1948 the Arab refugees were encourage to leave Israel by Arab leaders promising to purge the land of Jews Sixty-eight percent left without ever seeing an Israeli soldier.

10. The Jewish refugees were forced to floo from Arab lands due to Arab brutality, persecution and pogroms.

11. The number of Arab refugees who left Israel in 1948 is estimated to be around 630,000. The number of Jewish refugees from Arab lands is estimated to be the same.

12. Arab refugees were INTENTIONALLY not absorbed or integrated into the Arab lands to which they fled, despite the vast Arab territory. Of the 100 million refugees since World War II, theirs is the only refugee group in the world that has never been absorbed or integrated into their own peoples' lands. Jewish refugees were completely absorbed into Israel, a country no larger than the state of New Jersey.

13. The Arab - Israeli Conflict. The Arabs are represented by eight separate nations, not including the Palestinians. There is only one Jewish nation. The Arab nations initiated all five wars and lost. Israel defended itself each time and won.

14. The P.L.O.'s Charter still calls for the destruction of the State of Israel. Israel has given the Palestinians most of the West Bank land autonomy under the Palestinian Authority and has supplied them with weapons.

15. Under Jordanian rule, Jewish holy sites were desecrated and the Jews were denied access to places of worship. Under Israeli rule, all Muslim and Christian sites have been preserved and made accessible to people of all faiths.

16. The U.N. Record on Israel and the Arabs, of the 175 Secu-

95

rity Council resolutions passed before 1990, 97 were directed against Israel.

17. Of the 690 General Assembly resolutions voted on before 1990, 429 were directed against Israel.

18. The U.N was silent while 58 Jerusalem synagogues were destroyed by the Jordanians.

19. The U.N. was silent while the Jordanians desecrated the ancient Jewish cemetery on the Mt. of Olives

20. The U.N. was silent while the Jordanians enforced an apart-heid-like policy of preventing Jews from visiting the Temple Mount and the Western Wall. These are incredible times. We have to ask what our role should be. What will we tell our grand-children we did when there was a turning point in Jewish destiny, an opportunity to make a difference?

The "Palestinian" Myth (see Appendix 8)

The question often confronting me as I speak to Christian groups is…. "*But what about the plight of the Palestinians?*" I am not ashamed to clearly state that the land of Israel, plus much more, was promised by God in an everlasting covenant to the descendants of Abraham, Isaac and Jacob (**Gen 15:18** and **Psalm 105:6 - 11**)

The Europeans, in their quest to be fair and decent, have a genuine concern for the Palestinians, but their accusations against Israel are often unfounded, unbalanced, and verge on outright anti-Semitism.

The entire situation has been turned inside out by the world media. Let's look at the real facts concerning the Palestinians.

1/ Israel was first called Palestine by the Romans after they invaded and destroyed Jerusalem In AD 70. Satan used the pagan Roman Empire in an attempt to remove as much evidence of the existence of the true God as possible. The existence of the Jewish people and the nation of Israel, in turn declares the existence of the God of Israel. Therefore Satan's mission has been to kill the Jews and destroy Israel. Therefore even the name was changed to Palestine.

From that time on, Israel was called Palestine. The name was derived from the word 'Philistine', the race that Goliath belonged to and early Israel was often at war with. They also tried to change the name of Jerusalem to Aelia Capitolina.
Palestine has been ruled by Rome, by Islamic and Christian crusaders, by the Ottoman Empire and by the British after World War I. There is no Palestinian language. Palestinians are Arabs, indistinguishable from any other Arab group – Jordanians, Syrians, Lebanese or Iraqis.

The land that the Romans renamed 'Palestine' was inhabited by Jews, so therefore the real 'Palestinians' are the Jewish people The name Palestine was given to remove any connection to God, and I believe even calling Israel "Palestine" is an affront to the Lord.

2/ The Palestinians are simply Arabs. My friend and Christian brother in Yeshua, Salvatore, is an Arab Israeli. He has several relatives who are Palestinian Arabs. The only difference is that some of the family accepted to live in harmony with the Jews, when the UN created the State in 1948, and the others were encouraged not to. All of the Arabs who lived in the area that became Israel were given the choice to stay and live as Israelis, or to move on. And there was plenty of other Arab land nearby to move to, as well as an abundance of oil money to enable their fellow Arab nations to assist financially, if they really cared about their Palestinian relatives.

The Arabs have **650 times more** land than the Jews. God said that He would bless the descendants of Ishmael and He has. The Arabs were given the oil and the Jews got the oranges! As sweet as the Jaffa oranges are, I am sure the Jews would exchange the oranges for the oil any day.

In simple human terms it is jealously that is at the heart of the issue over the land of Israel. Hagar was jealous of Sarah, and the Arabs are jealous of this land that God gave to the Jews. Of course it is Satan that inspires this jealousy and uses the evil religion of Islam to inflame it.

"The Jews took no one's land" is the title of the most recent article by Arab-American Joseph Farah. "At no time did the Jews uproot Arab families from their homes," Farah writes in a brief overview of the last 150 years of history in the Holy Land, explaining that when Jews returned to their homeland, barely any Moslems were on hand to greet them.   (Arutz 7 article April 23rd 2002)

Excerpt from Farah's article: *"When Mark Twain visited the Holy Land in the 19th century, he was greatly disappointed. He didn't see any people. He referred to it as a vast wasteland."* The land now again called Israel was practically deserted.

By the beginning of the 20th century, Jews from all over the world began to return to their ancestral homeland – the Promised Land which Moses and Joshua had conquered almost four millennia earlier. A travel guide to Palestine and Syria, published in 1906, illustrates the fact that even when the Islamic Ottoman Empire ruled the region, the Muslim population in Jerusalem was minimal. The book estimates the total population of the city at 60,000, of whom 7,000 were Muslims, 13,000 were Christians, and **40,000 were Jews**...

And even though Muslims today claim Jerusalem as the third holiest site in Islam, when the city was under Islamic rule, they had little interest in it. As the Jews came, drained the swamps and made the desert bloom - Arabs followed. They came for jobs. They came for prosperity. They came for freedom. And they came in large numbers...

Then came 1948 and the UN partition. The United Nations proposed the creation of two states. One Jewish and the other Palestinian. The Jews accepted gratefully, but the Arab leaders rejected it with a vengeance and immediately declared war against the new state of Israel.

Several hundred thousand Arabs were displaced in this war. Not by Israeli aggression, but by the Arab leaders who urged all the Arabs to leave the area. In fact there are many historical records showing that the Jews urged the Arabs to stay and live with them in peace. But, tragically, they chose to leave and have been 'refugees' ever since.

3/ Israel followed the directives of the 1993 Oslo Peace Agreement and in 2000, PM Barak's government offered the Palestinian people **98%** of the land for their own state. If you were involved in a negotiation and someone offered you 98% of what

A SLOW COMING

you asked, if you are reasonable person, you would take it. But Arafat said "**NO**", and proceeded to direct his people to make war against Israel. The world's No 1 terrorist had not changed his spots!

As a result of Arafat personally directing and funding this 18 month war of terror against innocent Israelis, whose only desire is to live in peace in the land that God gave to their forefathers and God gave them back in 1948, more than 590 Israelis are dead, shot or blown to pieces as they sat in buses or in restaurants, and more than 1500 Palestinians are dead, most of them personally involved in making war against Israel.

So **what about the poor Palestinians?** What an absolute shame they have a demonically inspired killer as a leader! They could have had their state and more than 1500 of them would not be dead today if it wasn't for Yassar Arafat, arch-terrorist, cold blooded killer, and the 'darling' of the UN and European government leaders.

The truth of the matter is that Satan wants Jerusalem and specifically the Temple Mount, because he knows that is the only place Yeshua can return to. But the Devil can't have it - he will never get it, and the sooner ALL Christians realize and agree with that, the sooner true peace will come, when the Prince of peace returns to take up His throne in a Jewish Jerusalem, the capital of Jewish Israel.

As New Testament believers we all are called to be '**ambassadors of the Messiah**' (2 Corinthians 5:20) - be a good ambassador and boldly stand for the nation you have been grafted into. Pass this information on to your pastor, your family and friends and to your local news media. Tell them to tell the truth!

The World is at the Crossroads

Matthew 7:14 ...... *for narrow is the gate and difficult the way that leads to life and few there are that find it.*

On one hand the Lord tells us that it is His will that none perish (Matthew 18:14), but on the other hand He tells us that He has made some vessels for honour and some for dishonour.(Matthew 9:21). The conflict between Israel and the Palestinians rages on and the world is at a major crossroad.

The fulfilment of Zechariah 12:2-3 looms over the whole world at this very point in time. *Behold, I will make Jerusalem a cup of drunkenness* (Hebrew: a chalice of poison), *to all the surrounding peoples, when they lay siege against Judah and Jerusalem. And it shall happen in that day that I will make Jerusalem a very heavy stone for all peoples; all who would heave it away will surely be cut in pieces, though all nations of the earth gather against it.*

As we contemplate the events of the Al Aksa Intifada, it is incredible how fast the world has approached and even entered this crossroad. There are two ways to go. To take the road with Israel or to take the road against Israel. That is the surface issue. The real issue is taking the road with God or against Him, because it is He who brought the world through 6000 years of history to this point in time and to these crossroads which will divide the world and the Church, according where they stand with Israel.

Joel 3:2 *I will also gather all nations, and bring them down to the Valley of Jehoshaphat; and I will enter into judgment with them there on account of My people, My heritage Israel, whom they have scattered among the nations.*

A SLOW COMING

World history unmistakably testifies that the Lord keeps both His promises and threats. Genesis 12:3 *I will bless him who blesses you and I will curse those who curse you.*

Every great world empire that came against Israel was very quickly and harshly dealt with by Adonai Tzevaot (Lord of Hosts - the Hebrew word **tzevaot** means armies.) Babylon, Egypt, Medo-Persia, Greece and Rome were left, and still are mere shadows of the empires they once were, before making the tragic mistake of coming against Israel.

History also testifies that we Jews never learn from our mistakes. The Jewish people must learn that they can trust in **NO ONE** except the God of Abraham, Isaac and Jacob.

Psalm 81:13-14 *Oh that my people had hearkened unto me, and Israel had walked in my ways! I should soon have subdued their enemies, and turned my hand against their adversaries.*
And the Gentile nations are yet to learn not to put their hand against Israel, which God says is the apple of His eye.

Anti-Semitism is on the Rise

In March 2002, following the terror attack at a Netanya Passover celebration which claimed the lives of 29 innocent people, Israel finally took offensive steps to halt the attacks on Israeli citizens that had taken the lives of more than 450 Israelis in 18 months. What is most shocking to me, after the tragic loss of life on both sides, is the almost universal condemnation of Israel coming from every corner of the planet. I am convinced that it is not really Israel that they find offensive. They are offended to think that there is a Divine Being in Heaven who has ultimate authority and control over what happens in the world.

In this very late hour of the present age, with the closeness of Yeshua's return, which will mark the end of this age of man's self rulership, the spirit of Humanism has come in like a flood. And that Humanistic spirit hates the thought of having to submit to the Lordship of the true God.

A confrontation of gigantic proportions looms as the majority of the world continues to travel down the path that leads to destruction. Almost every world leader is sticking a finger in the apple of God's eye. Even those who claim to be Bible believing Christians seem to have taken the wrong turn at the crossroads of the Middle East.

Apart from the "Ruth" Christians, a rapidly growing number who are now realising the truth about God's plans and purposes for Israel and the Church, there are very few voices crying out on Israel's behalf.

The Church was virtually silent as 6 million Jews perished at the hands of the Nazis, and today there is still a 'deafening silence' from the majority of Christian pulpits.

Most of the Church had been similarly quiet as the suicide bombers have struck the Israeli people. In fact, of the few voices that are heard, many are crying out against Israel. But the Lord will have His day in the valley of Jehoshaphat.

On behalf of all the Jewish people and our fellow Israeli citizens, Josie and I want to commend each of you who have made the often costly decision of taking the narrow path to walk alongside the nation of people whom the Lord chose 4000 years ago to be His agents of redemption.

A SLOW  COMING

Keep up the great work and please continue to try to help others, including your pastors to see the truth concerning Israel and act upon it.

****

Chapter 9

The Name of God

Ever since the tragic terror attacks in the USA on September 11th 2001, we have seen an increase in the number of people praying to 'God'. My question is "which God are they praying to?" What is the name of their God?

Over the last several years we have an increase in 'interfaith' prayer meetings. Jews, Christians, Muslims, Hindus, Buddhists and others all praying to their 'God'. Later in this chapter, we will look in-depth at the Islamic god 'Allah'.

Who is the God of Abraham?

Gen 15:7 *And he said unto him, I am the LORD that brought thee out of Ur of the Chaldees, to give thee this land to inherit it.*

Throughout the Bible, where the English is translated as "LORD", the Hebrew is **"Yod Hey Vav Heh"**. The Strongs Hebrew/Greek Dictionary number is **3068 Yehovah** (Yeh-ho-vaw'); (the) self-Existent or Eternal; Jehovah .....

No one really knows how to pronounce **YHVH**, not even the Hebrew scholars, because there are no vowels in the original text. In English it is pronounced as Yahweh or Jehovah.

A SLOW COMING

As I have already said, 'God' is not His name. The word God is a generic title. If you assembled ten people and asked them to describe their 'God', they would probably all describe a different being.

I believe that the Jews and Christians made a serious mistake in replacing the name of the God of the Bible, with the generic terms, 'Elohim, Adonai, God or the Lord'.

These names are too vague, and leave it open for each person to decide who they are visualizing. If we had always called God by the name He gave to Abraham, many more people would be worshipping the true God.

What is His Son's name? (Proverbs 30:4)

In the English-speaking world, the Son of God is known as **Jesus Christ.** I am sure many people think that **Christ** was Joseph's and Mary's surname. His real name is **Yeshua** or **Y'shua,** which in Hebrew means **Salvation,** and He is the Christ or the Anointed One – the Messiah. Therefore He is Yeshua Ha Mashiach or Jesus the Christ.

To truly understand the terminology, we need to know the meaning of the names and words in their original language.

Hebrew		Greek		English
======		=====		======
Yeshua	=	Iesos	=	Jesus
Mashiach	=	Christos	=	Christ

****

Is Allah the God of the Bible?

The following interesting and informative article goes a long way towards explaining the reasons wo should not consider Allah and the God of Abraham to be the same. Part of the confusion is that there is only one word for 'god' in Arabic and that is "allah". In reality, Allah was the name of the pagan moon god of Mohammed's tribe; thus the lunar crescent in much of Muslim symbolism. While I don't doubt that many, if not most Muslims are peaceful people, I hope you will find this informative article useful in understanding the true nature of Islam, and why it allows the atrocities performed in its name.

Allah: The God of the Bible?
(An Article From Intercessors for America)

"Equality is an ideal that most people defend. And yet what is really meant is that equality is desired for one's self, not necessarily for the other person. Moslems want, and are granted, equality in the Western world to build mosques and win converts for Islam, but Christians are denied the right to preach the gospel in Islamic countries."

The Persian Gulf War brought a flood of TV images of the Arab world and Islam into millions of American homes. Many Americans, also very "religious" as Gallop polls repeatedly show, were sometimes deeply stirred by scenes of Islamic devotion and ritual.

This media barrage worked to reinforce the misguided belief in millions of Americans, including many Christians, that "Allah", the god of Islam is the God of Abraham, Isaac and Jacob, and the God and Father of our Lord Jesus Christ. Nothing is further from the truth.

A correct understanding of Islam is vital at this time because the Holy Spirit is challenging the Church toward global evangelism and church planting in an almost unprecedented way. Islam, which marshals hordes of spirits of antichrist and is propelled by barbarism, bloodshed, tyranny and perversion, now grips over 800 million souls worldwide. It is presently the dominating influence in more than 32 countries in the Middle East, Asia, Europe and Africa.

Christianity enjoys an Abrahamic and Hebraic Biblical root, but shares no Islamic heritage. Nor can the Bible be equated with Islam's "holy" book, the Koran, a compilation of "revelations" received from the "Archangel Gabriel".

Marius Baar, author of the excellent study, "The Unholy War", reminds us that God has made only two primary covenants: the Mosaic with Israel through Moses on Sinai, and the Messianic with the Church through the sacrifice of His Son on the cross. The New Testament admonishes the Christian to honour the Jewish people, the Messianic race and "root" of their faith. (Romans 11:18,20) But, there is no common destiny between Jews, Christians, Moslems or the practitioners of any other religion, except as individuals (Jew or Gentile, including Arab) repent of dead works (sin), put a personal faith and trust in the blood atonement of Jesus Christ, enter the New Covenant and worship Christ as Risen Lord and King. (Matthew 26:28)

While the Koran notes Jesus as the son of Mary and recognizes Him as a prophet and acknowledges some of His miracles, it unequivocally denies Him being the Son of God (Sura 9:30), denies Him being equal with God (Sura 5:17,75), denies that

He was crucified (Sura 4:157) and therefore does not even comment upon His Resurrection. This brings us to the matter of Allah, the god at the centre of each Moslem's "Faith." No "Faith" is possible to a Moslem apart from Allah, and the Koran terms all who refuse to put "Faith" in Allah to be hypocrites, infidels and renegades worthy of one thing, the sword: "Seize them and slay them wherever ye find them; and take no friends or helpers from their ranks." (Sura 4:89)

While the Arabic word "allah" does mean "god", in actuality Allah and the God of the Bible bear no resemblance. A look at the history of Islam's founder and "prophet, Mohammed," quickly clears away any confusion.

Mohammed, or Abul Kasem Ibn Abdullah, as he was first named by his Arab parents of the Quraish tribe, was born in Mecca, Arabia (now Saudi Arabia) in AD 570. His father, reportedly named Abdullah (servant of Allah), spoke the "magic" word Bismillah (in the name of Allah) before the birth to put his wife Amina's expected child under the protection of Allah, one of the 365 pagan deities worshipped in the Kaaba of Mecca and the god of the Quraish tribe, therefore the chief deity of Mohammed's family.

Thus, as Marius Baar states, "Mohammed was dedicated before his birth to the god of a religion whose founder he was to become."

As a young man, Abul drove camels in desert caravans and became a caravan master's orderly. These trips took him into Syria and he became familiar with the monotheistic religions of Judaism and Christianity and their distinctive worship of one god, not many. At 25, he married a wealthy widow of Mecca, Kadijah, 15 years his senior. He left the caravan trade, became a merchant in Mecca and spent much of his time in meditation. At 40, while meditating in a cave near Mecca, he fell into a trance and claims to have been visited by the "Archangel Gabriel" (familiar spirit?) who told him he was the messenger of Allah. He assumed a new name, "Mohammed," and began to proclaim Allah was the only god, and that he was Allah's prophet.

Worshipping many gods, the centre of Arab pagan worship was the Kaaba in Mecca (today Islam's most holy shrine). In Mohammed's day, 365 gods were worshipped in the Kaaba. Allah was one of these and, as stated, was the chief god of the Quraish tribe, Mohammed's family lineage. In the Kaaba was mounted the "Black Stone." Among these idols, the "true" god, this stone god, surpassed them all. While human sacrifice was no longer made to it, animal sacrifice was. This stone god was considered so mighty that it made Mecca unassailable.

Mohammed and his band of followers preached, mounted raids and fought to eliminate worship toward the other idols at Mecca, and to elevate their god Allah as the only god. The culmination of this process was documented by Konrad Meyer in his 1975 study, "The Middle East at the Crossroads": "Mohammed, during a sacrificial feast in the Kaaba in Mecca, stood up, pointed to the Kaaba and cried, 'La alla illa allahu!" (There is no allah, except he be Allah.) This utterance of Mohammed's, changed into 'La illahilla Alla' There is no god but Allah, became the Islamic confession of faith." Thus enshrining Allah to the Black Stone (actually a meteorite), Mohammed proclaimed it held power to take away man's sins when kissed, and obligated every devout Moslem to make a pilgrimage (Hajj) to the Kaaba and this stone idol at least once in his lifetime. (Sura 22:26 37) This religious pilgrimage (Hajj) is one of the "Five pillars of

Islam." The other four are: the Kalima, the verbal declaration that "Allah is the most high god;" praying five times daily with bowing toward Mecca; the giving of alms for purification at the turn of the year, and fasting from dawn to sunset during Ramadan.

History shows the god of Islam, Allah, is definitively not the God revealed in the Bible. Allah is no more than one of the many Canaanite desert gods and stone idols with their attendant demons which were worshipped in the pagan Arab shrine at Mecca. (Deuteronomy 32:16 17; 1 Corinthinians 10:20) Allah was simply elevated to the position of highest demon, chief territorial spirit. As Konrad Meyer declared: "Those who com mit themselves to this spirit become prisoners of Satan." Islam then, is a demonic stronghold energized through a system of forced worship, fasting, legalism, and barbarism. Interestingly, Islam literally means "submission."

Noted Middle East observer Lance Lambert reminds us: "Islam has at its heart a triumphalism; a dogmatic belief that It must triumph." The dream of a vast and dominant Pan Arab Islamic empire remains the goal of Islamic fundamentalists. While homage to Allah has primarily been occurring in Western society via the Shriners' sects in Masonic temples, now the minarets of Moslem mosques penetrate the skylines of many European and American cities, including Washington, D.C. As Lambert warns: "The Islamic revolution is not just something that Christians can dismiss as some benign, benevolent expression of religiousness, it is something demonic."

How unfortunate that Abraham's son Ishmael, born of Hagar, Sarah's Egyptian maidservant, has become identified as founder of the present day system of Islam, rather than as patriarch of the Arab peoples. Abraham loved Ishmael and God

111

Himself declared that Ishmael, while "wild" and "living in hostility toward all his brothers," would become a "great nation" (Genesis 16:12). Most importantly, Scripture records that when Abraham died, both his sons "Isaac and Ishmael buried him." When Ishmael died he was "gathered to his people." In the Hebrew text, this is a specific phrase reserved for those who followed and died in the faith and covenants of Abraham. (Genesis 25:9,17)

How different the face of the Middle East and portions of the world might be if freed from Islam and the scorching tyranny of the desert demon, Allah. How great must be our Lord Jesus' desire to see His cousins, the Ishmaelite Arabs, enter and enjoy His Father's household! Let us intercede, engage in spiritual warfare and propagate the gospel to that end. Through prevailing prayer and the power of the Holy Spirit the multitudes held captive by Islam can be set free! Let it be soon Lord! Amen.

"As Christians, we can never join hands with Islam. Either we are on the side of Mohammed, who opposes Jesus Christ as the Son of God, and who calls faith in Him blasphemy, or else we are of the side of Jesus. The one excludes the other." Basilea Schlink

ISLAM means submission to god, allah. The name given to an adherent of Islam's religion is Muslim. Quran or Koran is Arabic for "the recitation". Caliph is the name of Arabic leader. Ayatollah is the name of the spiritual leader.

Three Islamic convictions:

1/ Economic success demonstrates Allah's pleasure. Oil is allah's gift to Muslims so they may achieve superiority and prove the supremacy of Islam.

2/ The Arab culture is the ideal expression of Islam.

3/ Islamic law declares that non Muslims do not belong to the House of Islam (Dar al Islam), but the enemy House of War (Dar al Harb).

Therefore, all non Muslims must be:

a) converted;

b) subjugated as a dhimmi; Dhimmis must wear identifiable clothing; live in marked housing; may not bear arms; may not be a witness in a legal court; may not be a guardian to Muslim child; or own a Muslim slave; or judge a Muslim in a court of law.

****

A SLOW COMING

Chapter 10

What Lies Ahead?

The Time of Jacob's Trouble

Both the prophet Daniel and Yeshua warned of a future time of great trouble known as "the time of Jacob's trouble" or "the time of great tribulation", that would precede the 2nd coming of the Messiah.

Jeremiah 30:7 *Alas! For that day is great, so that none is like it; and it is the time of Jacob's trouble, but he shall be saved out of it.*

Daniel 12:1 *At that time Michael shall stand up, the great prince who stands watch over the sons of your people; and there shall be a time of trouble, such as never was since there was a nation, even to that time.*

Matthew 24:21 *For then shall be great tribulation, such as was not since the beginning of the world to this time, no, nor ever shall be.*

A SLOW  COMING

Israel's history echoes with the cries of pain inflicted by a long line of demonically inspired tyrants who endeavoured to eradicate the Jewish people, and destroy the land of Israel.

Israel's Greatest Enemies

1449 BC   **Pharoah**

500 BC   **Haman**

187 BC   **Antiochus Epiphanes**

0   **King Herod**

AD 1939   **Adolf Hitler**

AD 2000   **Yasser Arafat**

AD ????   **The Anti-Christ**

Egypt and the Pharoah

The Lord heard the cries of Hebrew slaves and sent His appointed vessel, Moses to deliver His people from the cruel Pharaoh. Pharaoh did his best to thwart the plan of God, but his magicians were no match for the Lord. He set the Hebrews free to pass through the dry bed of the Red Sea and to finally enter the land He promised to Abraham 430 years earlier.

Haman

The next tyrant who tried to destroy the Jews was Haman. We read the account of this in the book of Esther. This event, remembered in the Jewish festival of Purim, takes place in ancient Persia (Iran). Haman failed and it was he who hung from the gallows he had constructed to hang Mordecai.

Antiochus Epiphanes

In the 2nd century BC, it was the turn of Greek-Syrian general Antiochus. He banned the keeping of the Sabbath and the Holy festivals, outlawed circumcision, and desecrated the Temple by sacrificing a pig on the altar. The Lord raised up the Macabee brothers to be Israel's deliverers on this occasion.

In 176 BC Judas Macabee and his brothers revolted against Antiochus. God empowered the Macabees to overwhelm the might of the Greco-Syrian empire. Antiochus was defeated and Israel lived on.

King Herod

One hundred and seventy years later, as God prepared to send His own Son, Yeshua as the Messiah / Redeemer of the entire Human race, Satan again foreknew the plan. He inspired King Herod to murder all the two year old boys in Bethlehem in a desperate attempt to prevent the One who had been born 'King of the Jews' from carrying out His plan of redemption.

A SLOW  COMING

Hitler and the Holocaust

Nearly 2000 years later, again Satan must have known about the imminent rebirth of the nation of Israel, so he found yet another suitable vessel to carry out his evil deeds. Satan must have been very busy as the young Adolf Hitler grew up, seeing to it that he suffered deep rejection. Then spending much of his youth living with an uncle who owned an occult bookshop, the young Adolf Hitler was a prime candidate to be used by the Devil in a further attempt to annihilate the Jewish people and put a stop to the main event of God's end-time plan. Hitler failed and the nation of Israel rose from virtual death in May 1948 and the prophetic clock, stalled since AD 70, began ticking on its final countdown to the imminent return of the Lord.

Yassar Arafat

Yassar Arafat, leader of the PLO (Palestine Liberation Organisation), and subsequently, the chairman of the Palestinian Authority, is the 'father' of modern terrorism. He is personally responsible for the invention of such acts of terror as aircraft hijackings, and aircraft being blown up on the ground and in the air. Since the signing of the Oslo Peace Agreement in 1993, and the Camp David Accord in 1995, Arafat has been the ultimate authority behind dozens of bus and restaurant bombings in Israel, costing the lives of hundreds of innocent Israeli citizens.

In turning down PM Ehud Barak's offer of 98% of the disputed territories, Arafat brought war on the Israelis and the Palestinians, and confirmed his place in this list.

Finally the Anti-Christ

I believe that as we approach the "*great and awesome Day of the Lord*" (Joel 2:31) we will see a final attempt by Satan to destroy Israel and the Jewish people. This time it will be Satan's masterpiece - the Anti-Christ. It is his last chance to abort the prophesied Word of God, and thus prevent the kingdom of God finally being established upon the earth. Satan knows that the Lord's return will bring about his total and eternal defeat.

This line of evil characters all had one thing in common (apart from trying to destroy the Jews). They all failed. But because these men all failed, do you think that Satan has given up? It is a difficult thought for a Jew to consider, but I believe the Devil will try one more time to annihilate the Jewish people. There is another Holocaust ahead!

We can see it in scripture.

Dan 12:1 *"At that time Michael shall stand up, the great prince who stands watch over the sons of your people; and there shall be a time of trouble, such as never was since there was a nation, even to that time."*

Rev 7:14 *And I said to him, "Sir, you know." So he said to me, "These are the ones who come out of the great tribulation."*

Matt 24:21-22 *"For then there will be great tribulation, such as has not been since the beginning of the world until this time, no, nor ever shall be. And unless those days were short-ened, no flesh would be saved; but for the elect's sake those days will be shortened."*

A SLOW  COMING

This last tribulation won't just be tribulation for the Jewish people. The Devil will also loose his wrath upon the other people he utterly hates, the Church of Messiah Yeshua.

Jeremiah 30:7 Alas! For that day is great, so that none is like it; and it is the time of Jacob's trouble, but he shall be saved out of it.

The Bible calls it the time of Jacob's trouble. Jacob is Israel, but Christians are grafted into Israel, grafted into Jacob, and that means grafted into 'Jacob's trouble' also.

This is not something to be afraid of. On the contrary, it will be a time when the people of God will rise up to be united in the Messiah, Jew and Gentile, to be the people God destined us to be.

Are You Ready for the Coming Tribulation?

Are you ready to stand in the time of great trouble? Now is the time to get yourself prepared to be a hero for the Lord. Many Christians believe that the Church will be taken out before the trouble begins, but we will see in an upcoming chapter concerning the timing of the Rapture, that this 'escape' theology seems to be opposite to what the Bible is saying.

We need to be prepared, as Noah was, to 'ride out the storm' that is about to hit the earth. A few years ago I heard a Messianic Jewish brother, Joel Chernoff, say this: "Failure to prepare is preparation to fail." In English we have a saying, "To be forewarned is to be forearmed."

*Daniel 11:32 ... the people that **do know** their God shall be strong, and do exploits.*

Do you want to be one of those who will be strong and do great exploits for God?   Well, **now** is the time to get prepared.

We need to be prepared physically, emotionally and most of all, we need to be prepared spiritually. We need to **know** our God, having both our feet placed firmly upon the 'Rock of Ages'.

Will There be a Third Temple?

As I speak at seminars and church meetings, the question that is most regularly asked is in reference to the building of the 3rd Temple.

Firstly, the next Temple to be built will be the '4th Temple', as we the Believers in Yeshua (Jew and Gentile) are the living stones of the 3rd Temple of the Lord.

I believe that the Jews will rebuild the Temple, right there on the Temple Mount, on the very spot where the Dome of the Rock mosque currently stands.

The primary reason for my argument for the rebuilding of the Temple, is that Yeshua will soon return to the Earth, to rule for 1000 years. He is the King of Kings, and kings live in castles or palaces. There is only one place where the King of Kings can rule the world from - God's 'castle' on the Temple Mount in Jerusalem.

The Temple of the Lord has stood there on top of Mt Moriah twice before. This is a very special spot to the Lord. It is the specific location on earth where God has chosen to dwell when He dwells among us.

121

A SLOW COMING

2 Chronicles 7:12 *Then the LORD appeared to Solomon by night, and said to him: "I have heard your prayer, and have chosen this place for Myself as a house of sacrifice."*

v16 *"For now I have chosen and sanctified this house, that My name may be there forever; and My eyes and My heart will be there perpetually."*

The other strong scriptural evidence for the imminent rebuilding of the Temple is even before Yeshua returns to take His rightful place there, the anti-Christ will set himself up as the Messiah.

2 Thessalonians 2:3-4 *Let no one deceive you by any means; for that Day will not come unless the falling away comes first, and the man of sin is revealed, the son of perdition, who opposes and exalts himself above all that is called God or that is worshipped, so that he sits as God in the temple of God, showing himself that he is God.*

Will the Jews rebuild the Temple? I believe that the answer to that question is a resounding YES! Much of the special Temple furniture and implements have already been recreated as have the priestly garments.

The Red Heifer

One major obstacle has also recently been overcome. For Temple sacrifices to begin, the ashes of a red heifer are required to purify all of the Temple implements. Red heifers have not existed for a long time. However we are living in the day of genetic engineering and an Orthodox rabbi has been working together with a Texas rancher. Together they managed to take some DNA from some part of the remains of a red heifer found in Jerusalem, and through genetic engineering, they produced a red heifer.

The baby cow was carefully nurtured and inspected to make sure it was 'kosher'. Unfortunately as it developed, four white hairs were found on its tail. This disqualified this animal, but more DNA was taken from it. I have heard there is now a whole herd of baby red cows being raised under careful supervision.

This should tell us that the Jews are serious about rebuilding the Temple. There are many scriptures that seem to say that Levitical sacrifices will be restored in the millenium rule of Yeshua on this earth - a 1000 year reign from a Jewish built Temple, on the Temple Mount.

A SLOW COMING

Chapter 11

Aliyah - A Holy Work of God

"Aliyah" is the term used to describe the return of the Jewish people to their homeland. In Hebrew the word 'aliyah' means **to 'go up'.** That is what Jews do when they return home - they go **UP** to Israel. Some go **up** to Ashdod, some go **up** to Tel Aviv, some go **up** to Haifa and some go '**all the way up**' to Jerusalem. Once you arrive in Jerusalem, there is no place you can go more **up** to - apart from Heaven that is! The noun for a female Jew who makes Aliyah, is 'Olah'. Interestingly this same word means a 'burnt offering'.

As one who made Aliyah from beautiful, tranquil New Zealand 10 years ago, I can tell you that living in Israel at times, I have felt like an Olah - a burnt offering, but Josie and I don't regret our decision to obey the Lord's directive to make Aliyah.

Aliyah is Holy - Holy to the Lord. It is His idea. Throughout the books of the prophets, Isaiah, Jeremiah and Ezekiel, the Lord speaks about Aliyah. There are literally hundreds of verses that speak about it.

A SLOW  COMING

Here are just a few of the hundreds of Aliyah verses.

Jeremiah 16:14-16 *"Therefore behold, the days are coming,"* says the LORD, *"that it shall no more be said, 'The LORD lives who brought up the children of Israel from the land of Egypt,' but, "The LORD lives who brought up the children of Israel from the land of the north and from all the lands where He had driven them." For I will bring them back into their land which I gave to their fathers.*

Isaiah 5:26 *He will lift up a banner to the nations from afar, and will whistle to them from the end of the earth; surely they shall come with speed, swiftly.* (More than 5 million Jews have come to Israel in the last 100 years.)

And He does not mean some of those from Russia and the Ethiopians with a few from the West thrown in. The Lord means for **ALL** the Jewish people to come home from every corner of the earth.

Ezekiel 20:40 *"For on My holy mountain, on the mountain height of Israel,"* says the Lord GOD, *"there all the house of Israel, ALL of them in the land, shall serve Me;"*

I have heard many Christians speak against the nation of Israel, saying that because the majority of Israeli Jews are still unredeemed, this present form of Israel cannot be the one prophesied.

I strongly suggest that 'Christians' like this read the Bible before making such foolish statements. Here is the process - first God will bring them home, **THEN** He will clean them up.

Ezekiel 36:23-28 "And I will sanctify My great name, which has been profaned among the nations, which you have pro-faned in their midst; and the nations shall know that I am the LORD," says the Lord GOD, "when I am hallowed in you before their eyes. For I will take you from among the nations, gather you out of all countries, and bring you into your own land. Then I will sprinkle clean water on you, and you shall be clean; I will cleanse you from all your filthiness and from all your idols. "I will give you a new heart and put a new spirit within you; I will take the heart of stone out of your flesh and give you a heart of flesh. I will put My Spirit within you and cause you to walk in My statutes, and you will keep My judg-ments and do them. Then you shall dwell in the land that I gave to your fathers; you shall be My people, and I will be your God."

Aliyah is a sign. It is a sign that the return of the Lord is just ahead of us. Yeshua is coming back to the Jewish people back in the Land that God covenanted to Abraham, Isaac and Jacob (Psalm 105:6 -11) and ready to welcome the Messiah to Jerusa-lem with the words that will open the gates of Heaven to re-lease Him to come (Acts 3:21) "**Baruch Ha Bah B'Shem Adonai**" (Matthew 23:39).

And He is coming back to Israel, not Palestine; to a united Jerusalem under Jewish control. The process is well under way - Israel is back as a nation, more than 5 million Jews are home, and there are more than 80 Messianic congregations in Israel who sing that song - **Baruch Ha Bah B'Shem Adonai.** And the Lord says that it is a banner - a sign. Not a sign for the Jews, but a sign to the nations.

Isaiah 11:11-12 *It shall come to pass in that day that the LORD shall set His hand again the second time to recover the rem-*

nant of His people who are left, from Assyria and Egypt, from Pathros and Cush, from Elam and Shinar, from Hamath and the islands of the sea.   He will set up a <u>banner for the nations,</u> and will assemble the outcasts of Israel, and gather together the dispersed of Judah from the four corners of the earth.

Aliyah is a sign to the world that the Son of God is about to return to rule the world from Jerusalem. That is why the Devil hates Aliyah. That is why much of the world and sadly many Christians are opposing the return of the Jews to the Land that is rightfully theirs.   The places that the world and the UN calls "the occupied territories" were given to the Jewish people as an eternal promise.

Psalm 105:9-11 *The covenant which He made with Abraham, and His oath to Isaac, And confirmed it to Jacob for a statute, to Israel as an everlasting covenant, Saying, "To you I will give the land of Canaan as the allotment of your inheritance."*

This is the root of the problem in the Middle East. Satan is using the Muslims to try to prevent the Jews living in their own land.

If Christians really mean it when they say "Maranatha" (Come Lord Jesus), then they must get involved in Aliyah. It is the plan of God for Gentile Christians to work with Him as He brings the Jews home. It is your calling as a Gentile Christian.

Isaiah 49:22 *Thus says the Lord GOD: "Behold, I will lift My hand in an oath to the nations, and set up My standard for the peoples; they shall bring your sons in their arms, and your daughters shall be carried on their shoulders;"*

Many Christians are already involved. Christian organisations like Ebinezer, Exobus, the ICEJ, Exodus, CFI and others have literally brought hundreds of thousands of Jews home to Israel over the last 25 years. On buses, ships and planes. If you are not involved, Josie and I want to encourage you to pray and seek the Lord as to how He wants you involved. Do it today!!!

Time is short - Satan is busy preparing another Holocaust. The last few weeks have seen a dramatic increase in anti-Semitism all over the world.

Jeremiah 16:16 *"Behold, I will send for many fishermen," says the LORD, "and they shall fish them; and afterward I will send for many hunters,"*

Christians must wake up to the holiness of Aliyah, and so must many Messianic Jews. There are hundreds of thousands of Messianic Jews all over the world who are very comfortable where they are. They may pray for Israel, they may send finances to Israel, but the Lord wants their bodies in Israel. Sadly, they have no vision for Aliyah. And many Messianic pastors have no vision for Aliyah. They are keen to see new Jewish believers coming into their congregations, but they do not want to see them leave - for Israel.

This is very, very sad. I once heard a Messianic Jewish brother, who was a pioneer in the Messianic movement, say that of all people, Messianic Jews should realise that God wants us back where we belong - in ISRAEL. All Messianic congregations should be 'staging posts', points of departure for the ancient homeland.

Please intercede with us as we pray for the Church and the Messianic Jews to wake up to Aliyah - it is of God and it is Holy.

A SLOW  COMING

Intercessors for the Restoration of Israel (I.R.I)

In light of the importance of Aliyah and the fulfillment of the prophecies concerning Israel's restoration, my wife Josie sensed the Lord speaking to her during 2001, prompting her to establish an international network of committed mature intercessors, to specifically focus intercession on Aliyah (return of Jews to Israel). Combined with that, the ministry also concentrates on specific focused intercession for salvation of Jews in Israel and around the world, and the maturity and growth for the body of Messianic believers, both in Israel, and for those called to take the Word of the Lord out of Zion, and be a light to the nations (Isaiah 49:6).

These three areas are all prophetic keys to the Lord's return and their completion will hasten the day of His coming.

If you sense the Holy Spirit directing you to be a partner in this intercession network, please email Josie at:

kiwi@netvision.net.il   - (n.b. this is an email network only)

****

Chapter 12

The Timing of the Rapture

The subject of the timing of the Rapture of the saints is always guaranteed to ignite a debate. Within Church doctrine, there are four main positions.

1/ No Rapture of the Church
2/ Pre-tribulation Rapture
3/ Mid-tribulation Rapture
4/ Post-tribulation Rapture

Many leaders totally avoid the topic of the Rapture. They don't believe it is an important enough issue to risk the division that discussion tends to create. However, I beg to differ, I believe that the existence of Israel unmistakably places us in the latter days. If this is indeed the case, a correct understanding of the end-time is essential. The Body of Messiah needs to be prepared for what is about to take place in the world. If the pre and mid-tribulation doctrines prove to be wrong, then many Christians who were expecting to be raptured may find themselves totally unprepared to survive the tribulation.

A SLOW COMING

The Lord has called us to be His fellow-workers. Therefore we need to know what lies before us, so that we can invest our lives in the work of the kingdom. Let us also remember that Jesus rebuked the people of His day for being able to discern the weather from the signs in the sky, but not being able to discern the signs of the times in which they lived. (Matthew16:3) I want to take a scriptural look at this controversial subject.

1/ No Rapture of the Church

I believe that 1 Thessalonians 4:16 shows the 'no-Rapture' option to be unscriptural. Some Bible teachers have quoted 1 Corinthians 15:51 to also support the Rapture. However, if we desire to rightly divide the Word of God, this verse on its own does not speak of a rapture. The verse simply states that we will all be changed in a moment of time, even the dead will be brought back to life. Taken in tandem with 1 Thessalonians 4:16, the Corinthian scripture may point to the Rapture, but standing alone it does not.

2/ Timing of the Rapture

That leaves the other three doctrines to discuss. The Bible also teaches that every word should be established by the word of two or three witnesses (Matthew 18:16). I am going to give you more than three scriptures that witness to the true timing of the Rapture.

i) Acts 3:21 *"whom heaven must receive until the times of restoration of all things, which God has spoken by the mouth of all His holy prophets since the world began."*

According to this verse, Jesus is being restrained in heaven until the prophecies are fulfilled. The prophets spoke of Israel's scattering and latter day restoration of the nation of Israel and the re-gathering of the Jewish people to the land of their fore-fathers. (Deuteronomy 30:3 / Jeremiah 30:3) Both Hosea (Hosea 3.5) and Jeremiah (Jeremiah 30:9) prophesy of the Jewish people serving **David their King.**

King David was long dead when these words were written. It is obvious that this is a prophetic statement referring to Israel one day serving the Messiah. Acts 3:21 tells us that it will have to be fulfilled before Yeshua is released from Heaven. Romans 11:26 says that one day all *Israel will be saved..*

ii) Romans 11:15 *For if their being cast away is the reconciling of the world, what will their acceptance be but life from the dead ?*

The ultimate *"life from the dead"* surely must be the resurrection of the dead as the last shofar (trumpet) blast announces the return of the Lord. (1 Thessalonians 4:16) According to Romans 11:15, that event is a result of the natural Jewish branches being grafted back into their own olive tree.

iii) Matthew 23:39 Yeshua said to the Jews in Jerusalem *"You won't see me again until you say Blessed is He who comes in the name of the Lord."*

Revelation 1:7 *Behold! He is coming on the clouds and every eye will see Him, even those who pierced Him.*

Taking both of those verses together, we can deduce that if Yeshua said that the Jews won't see Him again until they are ready to welcome Him back, then no one will see Him until the Jews welcome Him back.

133

A SLOW COMING

iv) Matthew 24 I agree that some Bible verses can be used to support the pre or mid-tribulation doctrines, but Matthew 24 should put any debate over the timing of the Rapture to rest. The disciples asked Yeshua, *" What will be the sign of Your coming and the end of the age?"*

Yeshua then systematically answers their question. I believe the only legitimate way to rightly divide this chapter is to read through it in the order that the Lord spoke it out. Let's take an overview of His answer.

v 5   *Many will come in My name*

v 6   *You will hear of wars and rumours of wars*

v 7   *For nation will rise up against nation and there will be famines, earthquakes and pestilences in various places*

v 8   *All these are the beginning of sorrows*

v 9   *Then they will deliver YOU up to TRIBULATION and KILL you and you will be hated by all nations for my names sake*

v 13   *But he who endures to the END will be saved*

v 15   *Therefore when YOU see the abomination of desolation as spoken by the prophet Daniel, standing in the Holy place (let him who reads understand)*

v 21   *Then there will be GREAT TRIBULATION, such as has not be seen since the world began*

v 22   *Unless those days were shortened, no flesh would be saved, but for the elect's sake those days will be shortened.*

v 30   *Then the sign of the Son of Man will appear in Heaven, and all the tribes of the earth will mourn and they will see the Son of Man coming on the clouds of heaven with power and great glory. And he will send His angels with a great sound of a Shofar*   (this lines up with 1 Thessalonians 4:16)

v 36   *But of that day and hour, no-one knows.*

v 40   *Then two men will be in the field; one will be taken and the other left. Two women will be grinding at the mill; one will be taken and the other left.*

This surely must be a picture of the rapture and it occurs at the END of the Lord's narrative, well after the GREAT TRIBULATION of verse 21

I used to prefer the mid-tribulation position, but by the Lord's words alone I was forced to reconsider and I arrived at the only possible Biblically correct position. According to Yeshua, the Rapture is immediately after the time He called **"the Great Tribulation"**.

Two more points that also confirm a post-tribulation Rapture:

(a) Ruth

A good number of today's Bible teachers see the book of Ruth as a prophetic picture of the end-time Church. Ruth the Gentile clung to Jewish Naomi. Ruth had done what all true Christians have done, whether they realise it or not, by making the God of the Jews, their God. But Ruth had gone even further. She said to Naomi, "Your people shall be my people, and your God shall be my God. Where you go I shall go, and where you die I shall die." (Ruth 1;16) This is a picture of total commitment and a picture of the end-time 'Ruth' Church standing with the Jewish people in the last days. 'Ruth' means friend, and Israel will need as many friends as possible in the time of the 'Great Tribulation'.

Ultimately, the whole world will come against Jerusalem and Israel in the final days. The non-Bible believing world will never be Israel's friend - quite the opposite will be seen to be true.

A SLOW COMING

Only the true Body of Yeshua will stand with Israel in the dark days ahead as both Jews and Christians pass through the days of Jacob's Trouble, standing united against the wrath of a Satanically inspired one world government and the false church, both of which are already being formed.

(b) Yeshua came the first time for the Jewish people

By His own declaration Yeshua came the first time for *the lost sheep of the House of Israel* (Matthew 15:24) and I believe that He will come for the House of Israel when He returns. The only difference is that this time there are millions of 'wild branches' who have been grafted into the 'Olive Tree' of Romans 11:17 that represents the House of Israel. God only has one house, one people. The Church does not stand separately as many Christians would believe. Paul commands us *not to boast against the (natural) branches, but remember that you do not support the root, the root supports you* (Romans 11:18).

Were it not for the fact that God has grafted the Church into the natural olive tree - the Church simply would not exist. **ALL** Christians are now *'fellow citizens'* of the commonwealth of Israel (Ephesians 2:11 - 19).

Yeshua is coming back for His bride - do you really believe that the Bride of the Jewish Messiah will be void of most of the Jewish people? Paul didn't believe so. In Romans 11:25 Paul tells us that a certain number of Gentiles are pre-destined for salvation and when that number is complete, then the Lord will supernaturally remove the veil that has blinded the eyes of the Jews and then ALL Israel will be saved (Romans 11:26).

Yeshua will not take His bride out until she is complete with Jews and Gentiles. The Jews have been blinded to the truth and have suffered dreadfully for the last 2000 years, so that you dear reader, if you are a Gentile, could be grafted in. That is why Paul also says in Romans 15:27 that it is your duty to bless the Jewish people in material ways. You are called to be a 'Ruth' in this time that you have come to the kingdom. Any other opinion, or the desire to escape the time of Jacob's Trouble, leaving the Jewish people behind to go through it by themselves, is un-scriptural, and in the light of the above scriptural evidence, must be seriously reconsidered.

****

A SLOW COMING

Chapter 13

What Part Can We Play ?

Let us take a look at what we can do practically to fulfill God's call to the Church to co-labour with Him as He completes the restoration of Israel.

1/ Prayer and Intercession

Let us review the situation. We are all branches grafted into the trunk of the olive tree - ISRAEL. Most of the natural branches are still broken off and lying spiritually dead on the ground. The Church has been predominantly made up of the grafted in branches for nearly 1900 years, and has been either looking upwards waiting to see the Lord coming back or looking sideways at each other, but almost never looking back down the tree upon which they sit. If they would look down they would see the arch enemy of Israel (and the Church) standing at the base of the trunk, with an axe, trying to chop the tree down. If the tree falls, the natural branches and the grafted in branches die.

We have the luxury of knowing the end of the story, that the OLIVE TREE survives, but it is up to us to pray towards that end. Only the natural Jewish branches who believe in Yeshua, and the grafted in Gentile branches are in a covenantal position with God to be able to do that!!! The Lord is looking for a church of Elijahs, to pray and intercede, *to weep between the porch and the altar*, to cry out *"spare your people, O Lord!"*

2/ Evangelism

We all know the story of the Prodigal Son. Now it is the elder brother who is the prodigal. The younger brother, the Church, has been living in the house of the Father while the elder brother, the Jewish people, have been out there squandering their wonderful inheritance. But the Father wants his older son to come home to Him. He is waiting to see **Israel** running up the path towards His house. Don't you think it would please the Father to see His other son, the Church searching the highways and byways of this world looking for his brother, to gently pick him up and bring him home. What a day that will be - it will be **LIFE FROM THE DEAD.**

Romans 1:16 *For I am not ashamed of the gospel of Christ, for it is the power of God to salvation for everyone who believes, for the Jew first and also for the Greek.*

It is time for all believers to be obedient to this scripture and begin to make serious efforts to share the Gospel with the Jewish people. This needs to be applied at a personal level, at congregational level and at the evangelistic organisational level.

I am not suggesting that you go and stand on a soapbox outside the local synagogue with your Bible. The Jewish people have been verbally and physically abused enough for 2000 years in the name of Yeshua. Pray for divine appointments and make the most of them. Learn how to be effective in witnessing to Jewish people. Please feel free to request a copy of our teaching **Helpful Tips for Jewish Evangelism.**

If you live by, or work with Jewish people, pray for them, be a friend to them, take every opportunity to share your experiences about the God of Israel with them. Gently and lovingly bring them home to the Father's house. Tell them their Abba in Heaven loves them and is waiting for them to come home to Him. But they also need to hear that the only way to do this is through repentance and by inviting Yeshua to be their Lord and Saviour. Share Old Testament scriptures that talk about God's love for the Jewish people and the verses that clearly point to Yeshua as Messiah.

3/ Financial assistance

If you are not Jewish, but you have been saved by the blood of the Jewish Messiah, then the following verse is speaking to you.

Romans15:27 *It pleased them indeed, and they are their debtors. For if the **Gentiles** have been partakers of their spiritual things, their **duty** is also to minister to them in **material** things.*

Derek Prince says in 'Who Owns the Land' *"How much spiritual inheritance would any of the rest of the nations have without Israel? Exactly nothing! We are all debtors to the Jewish people. GOD says there are ways we will have to pay back the debt."*

Clearly God expects the Church to support the Jewish people in material ways. Right now Israel needs your help as never

141

before. They can use clothing, furniture etc. and/or financial assistance to help meet the needs of our Jewish brethren going home. If you are willing to be obedient to the word of God, may I suggest that you contact the International Christian Embassy, Christian Friends of Israel, or Prayer For Israel representatives in your country. Remember, those who bless Israel will be blessed themselves. (Genesis 12:3)

I believe that the Lord also desires that we sow financially into the spiritual restoration of the Jewish people. You will read in chapter 16, how Christians should be blessing Israel financially.

If we all simply rise up and fulfil the purpose that God has destined for us, then the times of restoration will be completed and the Lord will then be able to answer our cry of ......
  " Maranatha "

****

Chapter 14

Calling the Ruths, Esthers and Elijahs

As I have ministered the message of this book in seminars and church meetings around the world, the Holy Spirit has often had me pray for the Ruth, Esther and Elijah anointings to be imparted to the people in the audience.

I believe that the lives of these three Bible characters are pictures of the Lord's calling to the 'end-time' Church. I want to take a closer look at the life and ministry of these three Bible heroes, and I believe that as you read this chapter, the Holy Spirit will speak to your heart and impart to you personally, one or more of these anointings.

Ruth

In Hebrew, Ruth means friend. Ruth was Gentile, a Moabite who became the daughter-in-law of Naomi, a Jewess. Naomi and her husband left Israel during a time of severe famine Years later her husband and two sons died and Naomi heard that the situation in Israel had improved. She gathered up her few belongings, and with her two daughters-in-law, Ruth and

A SLOW  COMING

Orpah, began the long journey back to her native Israel. Along the way Orpah had a change of heart and bid goodbye to Naomi and Ruth declaring that she was going back. Naomi told Ruth to go too, but Ruth 'clung' to Naomi and made this statement.

Ruth 1:16-17 *Ruth replied, "Don't urge me to leave you or to turn back from you. Where you go I will go, and where you stay I will stay. Your people will be my people and your God my God. Where you die I will die, and there I will be buried."*

Ruth didn't just talk the talk, she walked the walk – all the way to Israel, where she was happy to simply glean in the corners of the harvest field.

Israel is in trouble right now – more trouble than most Jews or Christians realize. The long line of tyrants who have tried to extinguish Israel's light and thus abort the prophecies has one more evil man waiting in the wings.

There will be a final attempt to rid the world of Israel and the Jews. Israel needs as many Ruths or friends as possible now and in the days ahead. And God has called the Church to be those Ruths.

Will you pay whatever price is required to fulfill this call and be a true 'Christian friend of Israel'?

Esther

Esther was a beautiful young Jewess who lived in Persia along with a great number of her people about 2500 years before the birth of the Messiah. Her story is recounted in the Old Testament book called by her name – Esther.

There was a servant of Satan by the name of Haman living in Persia at the same time. He schemed, lied, and manipulated the king into signing an edict which would have destroyed all of the Jewish people in the king's realm.

Esther 3:13   *And letters were sent by couriers to all the king's provinces to destroy, to kill, and to annihilate all the Jews, both young and old, women and children, in one day, the thir-teenth {day} of the twelfth month, which is the month Adar, and to seize their possessions as plunder.*

Because Esther had found favour with the King, a wise Jewish man by the name of Mordecai informed Esther that her people were in big trouble. He sent this message to Esther…

Esther 4:14-16 *For if you remain completely silent at this time, relief and deliverance will arise for the Jews from another place, but you and your father's house will perish. Yet who knows whether you have come to the kingdom for such a time as this?*

Not only was Esther a beautiful maiden, she had the spirit of God, the warrior spirit! She responded in the way that Mordecai had hoped for.

v15 *Then Esther told them to reply to Mordecai:*
v16 *"Go, gather all the Jews who are present in Shushan, and fast for me; neither eat nor drink for three days, night or day. My maids and I will fast likewise. And so I will go to the king, which is against the law; and if I perish, I perish!"*

The Lord is looking for Esthers today. Christians who, upon realizing Israel is in danger, will also be bold enough to stand up and protect Israel. Christians with that same warrior spirit that rose up in Esther, who will not be afraid to go in to the king, invited or not.

Who is the king today? The king may be your boss. He may be your pastor if your pastor is not for Israel. If you are a pastor or leader, he may be a higher official in your denominational organization. The king today may be a government leader or some media big-shot. He may be any prominent person who speaks or acts against the people whom you have made your people and the nation you have been grafted into and have become a 'fellow citizen' with – Israel and the Jewish people.

Will you be an Esther? Are you willing to pay the price? It may cost you your reputation. It may cost you your position. It may even cost you your life one day.

Elijah – The Prophetic Ministry

The original Elijah was a prophet of God who also lived about 2500 before the Messiah was born. He was a voice crying in the wilderness, crying out to the people with a message of national repentance. The Bible tells us that Elijah will come again to precede the 'dreadful' day of the Lord's coming.

Malachi 4:5 *Behold, I will send you Elijah the prophet before the coming of the great and dreadful day of the LORD.*

Hundreds of years later, another prophet of God was issuing the same warning to the people of Israel. John the Baptist was ministering in the spirit of Elijah.

Matthew 17:10-14 *And His disciples asked Him, saying, "Why then do the scribes say that Elijah must come first?" Jesus answered and said to them, "Indeed, Elijah is coming first and will restore all things. "But I say to you that Elijah has come already, and they did not know him but did to him whatever they wished. Likewise the Son of Man is also about to suffer at their hands." Then the disciples understood that He spoke to them of John the Baptist.*

John the Baptist's message to Israel was *"repent and prepare the way of the Lord. "*

The Lord is about to return and the verse in Malachi must be fulfilled again. But this time the message is not just for Israel. The whole world is standing on the edge of the abyss and needs to hear this message.

Time is short, the labourers are few and there is much work to do. This time, God is not seeking just one Elijah, but a Church full of Elijahs – voices crying in the wilderness "Repent and prepare for the coming of the Messiah."

The key to fulfilling the prophetic ministry of Elijah is found in the second line of the anointed song by Robin Marks - *"These are the days of Elijah, **declaring the Word of the Lord"**.* We need to be sure that what we are declaring or prophesying is indeed, and is only, the Word of the Lord.

Hebrews 4:12 *It is alive; it is powerful; and it is sharper than any two edged sword.*

A SLOW  COMING

Elijah – The Ministry of Intercession

In 1 Kings Chapter 18 we see Israel once again suffering from the effects of a severe drought. Elijah the prophet now turned to the ministry of intercession.

1 Kings 18:42 ……… *And Elijah went up to the top of Mt. Carmel; then he bowed down on the ground, and put his face between his knees.*

In those days, bowed down with one's head between one's knees, was the position a woman assumed to give birth. I believe that this is a picture of Elijah, the man of God, getting down into the birth position where he began to intercede and travail for the Lord to relent and send the rain.

We are called to weep and travail in intercession for 'our people'.

Joel 2:17 *Let the priests, who minister to the LORD, weep between the porch and the altar; let them say, "Spare Your people, O LORD……………"*

Who are the priests who '*minister to the Lord*' today? The answer is "we are" of course – Messianic Christians and Messianic Jews.

Who are 'our people'? If we are truly grafted into Israel and are now 'fellow citizens', then the Jewish people are 'our people'. But so are our family, our friends, our countrymen and the people of all nations are 'our people'.

Time is short and there are millions of Jews still on the 'wrong track', there are millions of people in churches who are still on the wrong track, and there are literally billions of Atheists, Buddhists, Hindus, Muslims, New Agers and others who are not even on the track at all. No wonder God desires us to be His co workers. There is a lot of work to do before the Lord can return.

Are you willing to play a part in God's end-time plans and purposes for Israel, the Church and the world?

Prayer: *Holy Spirit, I pray that You will touch the reader right now, as they finish reading this chapter. Release the Ruth, Esther and Elijah anointings upon those whom You are calling. Anoint them, appoint them, give them boldness and wisdom, and make every provision* ………

In Yeshua's mighty name – Amen!

****

A SLOW COMING

Chapter 15

Pray For the Peace of Jerusalem
Effective Fervent Prayer Avails Much - James 5:16

It has been on my heart for some time now, to make some suggestions regarding how we should be fulfilling our call to 'Pray for the Peace of Jerusalem'. I don't believe that it is as simple as praying for peace to come to Jerusalem. In fact, I feel that sort of prayer is a waste of precious time.

The Bible tells us there will be a 'Time of Jacob's Trouble' before the Lord's return. Peace will only truly come when the Prince of Peace comes to take up His Holy Throne In the city of the King, Jerusalem. Therefore we need to be very wise and pray for the changes to be brought about that will cause the gates of Heaven to open, thus releasing the King of Kings and the Lord of Lords to return to planet Earth to rule and reign for 1000 years from His Throne in Jerusalem.

A SLOW COMING

I am pleasantly surprised at the constantly growing number of Christians, answering the call to "Pray for the Peace of Jerusalem." We want to suggest the following guide to those serious about fulfilling the call to pray.

1/ General

By all means continue to pray as you have been in the past:

- for the political situation
- for the political leaders of Israel
- for protection against terrorist attacks
- for the salvation of the Jewish people in Israel and in the nations, and more importantly, as the Holy Spirit leads.

However I want to suggest the following is a more effective way to pray for Israel and the Jewish people.

2/ The Believers First

I believe that the Messianic Jewish part of the Body of Messiah is a direct fulfillment of Ezekiel 37:9 dry bones who have had the Spirit breathed into them. (In Hebrew the word for breath Ruach, is the same word as for spirit.) Surely as fellow members of the family of God, our primary prayer focus should be on the Messianic Body.

Here are some guidelines for prayer for our Messianic Jewish brothers and sisters.

a/ Unity The Messianic body is divided over a number of key issues. This is a ploy of the devil to keep us weak and ineffec-

live. We need to pray for UNITY for the leadership in Israel and indeed amongst Messianic Jewish leaders around the world. Also let us pray for UNITY and LOVE amongst the members of all the Messianic congregations.

b/ Protection

The Messianic Body stands as a beacon in today's world. We stand as a beacon to our own Jewish people, declaring that it is possible to believe in Yeshua and still be Jewish.

We also stand as a beacon to Christians, declaring that the Lord is indeed in the process of *RESTORING ALL THINGS AS HE SPOKE THROUGH THE HOLY PROPHETS* (Acts 3:21). The existence of Messianic Jews also stands as a beacon to the devil, declaring that the fact that we exist is evidence of the closeness of his demise.

In light of the above 3 points, can you see how much the devil must despise us and how intent he must be on aborting our destiny and calling?

When the Lord called King Cyrus to rebuild the Temple, the first thing Cyrus did was rebuild the altar. Next they rebuilt the Temple, then finally realizing that Israel still had enemies. Nehemiah commissioned the rebuilding of the wall. In our times, I believe the Messianic congregations house the altar, and the members of the congregations are the living stones of the rebuilt Temple.

What is needed again at this time is to rebuild the wall, a wall of prayer, around this fledgling sector of the Lord's Body. Messianic Jews represent a major milestone in the prophesied restoration of Israel, preceding the Lord's return.

A SLOW  COMING

It always has been the Lord's plan for the Church to be a primary partner in this. Will you be one of the Lord's co-workers on the 'wall rebuilding project'?

c/ A Prophetic Voice

God has always spoken to Israel through the voice of His appointed prophets. Israel needs to hear the Word of the Lord more than ever. In the midst of death and destruction from external attack and also from disasters within, there is no one speaking for God. Only a Messianic Jew can truly speak for God in Israel today. Please pray that the Lord will raise up a native born Israeli believer to be a voice crying in the wilderness here within Israel.

d/ A Light to the Nations

A major purpose of Israel's restoration to their Land and having the Ruach Ha Kodesh (Holy Spirit) breathed into us, is to fulfill the call of Exodus 19:6 and Isaiah 2:3 to be a light to the nations. Out of Zion Ministries has answered this call to take the Word out from Zion.

There is now a growing number of other Messianic Jews who are also answering this call on the Jewish people to go to the nations, but the majority have yet to receive the revelation. I believe there is a responsibility on Messianic Jews to be a light to the rest of the Church. *One day ten Gentiles will reach out to take hold of the garment of a Jew* (Zechariah 8:23). It is time for the Messianic Jews to mature and to be the light that we are called to be.

We need to pray for a rapid maturing of the Messianic Body, in

Israel and worldwide, that the leadership especially will have a revelation of the calling to the nations and will begin to prepare their congregations to send apostles to the nations.

The Church is called to provoke Jewish people to jealousy, but I believe first the Messianic Jews are called to provoke the Church to jealousy also, so that she will seek to be restored to her Jewish roots and then she will have what it takes to provoke the Jewish people. When all this comes to pass, the prophecies will be fulfilled, heaven will release the Lord to return and then at last peace will reign in Jerusalem.

e/ Church Leadership

There is one other area in which we can pray for the Peace of Jerusalem. Let us pray for pastors and church leadership to have a revelation of the relevance of the ongoing physical and spiritual restoration of Israel. Also that they would have a revelation of the need to take the Church back to her roots, her Jewish roots and that ultimately, the Church will be restored to the power and the glory of the 'Acts' Church of the 1st century. Then she will have what it takes to *"provoke the Jewish people to jealousy"*.

✻✻✻✻✻✻✻✻✻

A SLOW COMING

Chapter 16

How to Bless Israel Financially
(Unless the Lord builds The House?)

The Church is waking up to discover a major key in the Word of God. It is a key that releases the full blessings of the Lord. In Genesis 12:3, the Lord tells Abraham that *He will bless those who bless the seed of Abraham.*

Here is a radical, literal promise not to be removed by spiritualizing the word. We must allow God to speak for Himself. When the God of Abraham declared those words, He was referring to the physical descendants of Abraham through Isaac (Genesis 21:12 *in Isaac your seed shall be called*), and Jacob who later became Israel (Genesis 32:28), very obviously the Jewish people.

The restoration of secular Israel on May 14th 1948 was a miracle. The return of the five million plus Jews who have come home to Israel, and continue to come daily, is also supernaturally inspired and energised. Another supernatural restoration is currently taking place in Israel.

A SLOW  COMING

On the Biblical Festival of Shavuot (Pentecost) 2001, the leaders of a Haifa messianic congregation, Tents of Mercy, baptised 39 new believers as they celebrated the festival beside the Sea of Galilee.

This number of Jews coming to faith in their Messiah has not been seen since the early days of the Church in the first century. Israel's rebirth and ongoing restoration has brought about a vivid dramatic revelation to many Bible believing Christians that He is not yet finished with Israel.

Many now agree with Paul as he states emphatically in Romans 11:1, *"Has God finished with Israel? Certainly not!"* Hundreds of thousands of Jesus' followers have come to recognise the supernatural nature of this "resurrection from the dead" as pictured so graphically in Ezekiel's **"dry bones"** chapter 37. They have seen the hand of God directing the return of the more than five million Jews who have returned to Israel from every corner of the planet in the last one hundred years.

God clearly tells us through the Holy Scriptures that He has called the Gentiles to participate in the restoration of Israel and the Jewish people. The prophet Isaiah talks about the "wealth of the Gentiles"

Isaiah 60:11 *Therefore your gates shall be continually open; they shall not be shut day or night, that men may bring to you the wealth of the Nations*

Isaiah 49:22 speaks of the Gentiles carrying home the sons of Israel in their arms and the daughters of Israel on their shoulders.

This verse has been fulfilled by the numerous Christian ministries raising large amounts of money from other Christians all over the world, to finance the buses, ships and aircraft that have been carrying the returning exiles home. One such ministry alone has paid for more than 50,000 Jews from the former Soviet Union, to return to the homeland of their forefathers, Eretz Yisrael - Israel.

In Romans 15:27 Paul teaches the Romans that it is their duty to repay the Jewish people by way of material blessings for the spiritual blessings that they (the Gentiles) have inherited through faith in the Jewish Messiah.

In 1st Corinthians 3:9 the Lord calls us His *'fellow-workers'*. Therefore, it is scripturally right and proper for Christians to eagerly assist the Lord with financial resources as He continues to rebuild and restore Israel. I want to applaud those of you who are already doing so, and I want to encourage those of you who are not yet sowing financial blessings into the physical seed of Abraham, to prayerfully consider doing so.

Ultimately it will be to your own advantage. American Pastor Don Finto wrote in his recent book 'Your People Shall Be My People', "If the ancient promise in Genesis 12:3 is still true (and he believes it is), then no nation, people group, church or individual will ever receive their fullest blessing, until they learn to love and bless the Jewish people."

For those of you who would join with the millions of voices that have cried out "Maranatha Lord, come quickly" I draw your attention to Acts 3:21,

Acts 3:21 *whom Heaven must restrain until the times of restoration of all things as spoken by God through the mouth of His Holy prophets since the world began.*

From this one verse it would appear that Heaven will not permit the Lord's return until the prophecies of Israel's complete restoration are fulfilled. Ought we not do everything in our power to co-labour alongside the Lord as He transforms Israel into the nation of priests that she was destined to be?

The Bible teaches that *"unless the Lord builds the house, they labour in vain who build it."* A good idea may not necessarily be a 'God' idea. With regard to supporting Israel, I want to respectfully submit an example of well-intentioned 'labour' appearing to 'build God's house' yet lacking wisdom.

It is a fact that millions of dollars are being donated to secular and Orthodox Jewish causes by Bible believing Christians. I am not referring to donations made to organisations involved in Aliyah, (helping needy Russian and Ethiopian Jews come home).

Allow me to illustrate a phenomenon in which many Christians are involved. Recently I was in the office of an American pastor. He proudly began to show me photographs of a Yeshiva (Orthodox Jewish Bible school) that his church had donated hundreds of thousands of dollars to help build. These Yeshivas teach against Yeshua and the New Covenant, and are for now, enemies of the Messianic Jews. The same pastor is among many who donate large amounts of money to the Temple Mount Faithful, an organisation committed to rebuilding the Temple.

To some Christians that may sound like a good cause. However this organisation is viciously opposed to Messianic Jews and even accuses us of destroying Jewish souls in a way worse than the Nazis did.

They believe the existence of Messianic Jews in Israel is preventing the coming of the Messiah (1st coming) and they seek to eradicate us by whatever means necessary. And well-meaning but deceived Christians are helping to fund the Temple Mount Faithful!

I also heard of a Christian sending finances to the Yad L'Achim (the Hand of the Brothers), the anti-missionary organization that is behind most of the persecution of Messianic Jews in Israel.

We praise the Lord for every Christian who has a heart to bless Israel. However the above examples are just two of many in which those directly opposing Jesus' modern Jewish disciples are being funded at the expense of the Body of Messiah. So much more could be achieved in Israel, if we had the financial support of the greater Body of Messiah around the world.

Christians are called to be the Lord's fellow workers. What then are we doing working with the enemies of the Gospel? I want to encourage Christians to think carefully, and more importantly, to **pray** about how and where to invest their financial support of Israel and the Jewish people. The Lord has called you to the Kingdom for such a time as this, to play a specific part in His end-time purposes for Israel, the Church and the world.

Only He knows what that part is and the only way you will know is to ask Him.

Please feel free to contact Out of Zion Ministries, if you would like more information or if we can assist you in any way.

A SLOW COMING

Chapter 17

Living Stones Tours

Encouraging Christians to visit the Messianic Jewish Brethren in Israel

The current Palestinian Intifada has decimated tourism in Israel. Tourism is down 80%, inflicting major damage to the Israeli economy. We believe that the last days Church is called to be "RUTH" to Israel. Life in 98% of Israel is normal and as safe as before the current troubles began. So why are 80% of Christians cancelling their tours? Is it because of fear, based on misinformation, or is it because the secular tour operators are afraid to bring groups due to problems with insurance etc. Is it right that Christians be controlled by un-believers and prevented from fulfilling the Lord's will?

Whatever the reason, the Devil must be clapping his hands in glee. The "Ruths" are staying at home instead of coming to stand with Israel in her time of need. We have to pose the question "If the Believers are afraid to come now when there is a small risk, who will be a 'RUTH' to Israel when the BIG TROUBLE breaks out?"

A SLOW COMING

We at **Out of Zion** Ministries sense a call to inspire and assist Christians to continue with their plans to come to Israel in these days, Intifada or no Intifada. I have written the following article which I encourage you to give to any Pastors or friends or anyone you know who are or were thinking about coming to Israel, but may be having second thoughts or are unable to find a travel agent who is willing to organize the tour.

The second purpose of Living Stones Tours is to encourage Christians to connect with the Messianic Jewish Believers here in Israel. In more peaceful times, each year hundreds of thousands of Christians realize their dream of a pilgrimage to the Holy Land. For the majority of people, this is a once in a lifetime opportunity.

However, the majority of Christian tour groups are missing a key aspect of what God is doing in Israel in the times in which we live. This is a tragedy for all concerned and I see it as a ploy of the Devil to keep Christians and Messianic Jews apart. He does not want Christians to witness the miracle that is taking place in Israel today.

Acts 3:21 tells us that *"Heaven is restraining the Lord's return until the time of the restoration of all things as spoken by God through His holy prophets."*

Let's go to the book of Ezekiel, chapters 36 and 37 to discover what it was the holy prophets said.

Ezekiel 36:8 *"O mountains of Israel, shoot forth your branches for my people Israel are about to come"*
This scripture was fulfilled on May 14th 1948 as the modern nation of Israel was born in one day.

Ezekiel 37:4-6   *Prophesy to these bones and say to them, O dry bones, hear the word of the Lord, Surely I will cause breath to enter into you and you shall live. I will put sinews on you and bring flesh and cover you with skin and put breath in you and you shall live.*

In the last 100 years, more than 5 million Jews have come home to Israel from every corner of the Earth. These 5 million 'dry bones' are the fulfillment of the above prophetic scriptures.

Ezekiel 37:9 *"Prophesy to the breath, prophesy son of man, and say to the breath, Thus says the Lord God, Come from the four winds, O breath, and breathe on these slain that they may live"*

I believe that this scripture is currently being fulfilled in the amazing growth of the Messianic Jewish movement all over the world and more pointedly, in Israel. Since 1967, the number of Messianic Jewish congregations has grown from none to more than 400 world-wide and incredibly, there are now more than 80 Messianic congregations in Israel. This is nothing short of a 'modern miracle', as these congregations simply didn't exist 33 years ago!

I call the standard Christian Holy Land tours, **'Dead Stones Tours'**! Pilgrims are taken to many of the 'Holy' sites to see the remaining dead stones, where it is claimed that the Lord ministered 2000 years ago.

That's fine, but I have a vision to see these pilgrims offered **'Living Stones' Tours.** Tours which will visit the key 'Holy' sites but more importantly, we will also include visits to local Messianic congregations. Come and see what the Lord is doing in Israel today. Come and worship with us at our Sabbath services. We are also willing to provide half-day or evening seminars.

Everyone will be blessed. The local Believers will be blessed to know that our brothers and sisters in the nations care enough about us to visit us. The pilgrims will be blessed as they stand in the midst of hundreds of those 'dry bones' who have now returned to their Land and have come to know their Messiah. To see with their own eyes and to stand in the midst of the fulfillment of Bible prophecies.

Let us work together to see this change. Let us put a stop to the disappointment of the Israeli Believers, who see the thousands of buses, full of brothers and sisters in the Lord, drive by our meeting places, oblivious to the fact that we are here or that we even exist. What a shame to come all that way, only to miss it by just a few kilometres!

Out of Zion is prepared to assist you in any way we can to put together a **'Living Stones Tour'**. We are offering to help find accommodation in guesthouses operated by local Believers and to supply guides who are Messianic Jews. We can also arrange rental vehicles, buses and suggest which sites should be visited and which local Messianic congregations are open to visiting groups.

If you are interested, please write to us at the **Out of Zion Ministries** postal or email address.

Chapter 18

Repentance For Anti-Semitism

In Genesis 12:3 we see a major key to see the blessings of the Lord. *I will bless those who bless you.*

Following the promise of blessing, we see a serious warning, *"I will curse those who curse you."*

We have read much about the recent increase in anti-Semitism. Intense hatred based simply on someone's race, as with anti-Semitism, doesn't make sense unless you understand it from the spiritual perspective.

There are only two kingdoms in the world - the Kingdom of God, and the kingdoms of this world which are under the control of Satan. The Bible tells us that he is the god of this world (2 Corinthians 4:4) and that the whole world lies under his influence. (1 John 5:19)

Satan hates Israel, (and he similarly hates the true Church which it is grafted in to become one with Israel) because it represents God's Kingdom. Therefore it is natural that the spirit that pervades the whole world, which is under his influence, is an anti-Semitic spirit.

A SLOW COMING

Therefore a flame of anti-Semitism burns inside almost every human heart, shockingly even in the hearts of many people who consider themselves to be Christians. It is understandable that the world be against the Jewish people, but anti-Semitism does not belong in the Church. Anti-Semitism is a curse against the Jewish people, and according to Genesis 12:3, God curses those who curse Israel.

It is easy to get the spirit of anti-Semitism out, by a prayer of repentance. However in all of my Christian experience, I have never heard anyone counselling new believers or those with obvious curses on their lives, to repent of anti-Semitism. We are told that we need to repent of sexual sin, smoking, alcohol, drugs, stealing, occult involvement etc, but virtually never is anti-Semitism included in the repentance.

If we are honest, nearly all of us have had a wrong attitude towards the Jewish people at some time or other in our lives, before or even after we became Christians.

As I said at the beginning it is normal, because it is one of the primary spirits at work in the world. What else would we expect, when every Easter, from the time we are infants, we are told without proper explanation, that the Jews murdered Jesus.

If you have not already personally repented of anti-Semitism, then there may well be a curse over your life that is preventing the Lord's blessings being poured out. You need to repent.

And if you are one of the very few Gentiles who have never had a wrong attitude towards the Jews, then what about your father, grandfather and great grandfather? The Bible tells us that the sins of the fathers are handed down to the 3rd and 4th generations, maybe even beyond.

Exod 34:7 *Keeping mercy for thousands, forgiving iniquity and transgression and sin, and that will by no means clear the guilty; visiting the iniquity of the fathers upon the children, and upon the children's children, unto the third and to the fourth generation.*

There may be a curse over your entire family because of the anti-Semitism of your forefathers. You need to repent on behalf of your forefathers.

I want to pray and bless you, but you may not be able to receive the full blessing until the curse of anti-Semitism is broken off you.

I suggest you pray right now and ask the Lord to forgive you and your forefathers for any wrong attitudes you or they have harboured against the Jewish people. It is OK to tell a good Jewish joke, but many Jewish jokes are very distasteful and constitute anti-Semitism. You should repent of that also.

Take a few moments to pray, ask the Holy Spirit to show you any specific things you need to repent of ....

Now I will pray for you .... *Abba, I ask that you wash and cleanse by the blood of Yeshua, every person who has repented of anti-Semitism. Forgive them I pray and in the name of Yeshua, I break every curse that has come upon them and their families, by their own sin, or by the sins of their forefathers. Sickness, poverty, every curse is lifted off and replaced with the blessings of Abraham. Bless their health, bless their families, bless their finances, bless their spiritual lives ....*

In the name of Yehsua .... Amen

A SLOW  COMING

SALVATION PRAYER

In Isaiah 11:11 and 12, the Bible tells us that God has made Israel a banner to the Nations. What is a banner? A banner is a sign. The marketing world knows the power of advertising signs. And so does the spirit realm. God says that He has made Israel a banner or a sign to the Nations, or the Gentiles.

I believe that this sign says something like this .... **"This is God calling Earth. I am not dead - I am alive and at work in the world today. If you wan to see what I am doing, look at Israel. It is a sign that My Son is coming back to the Earth very soon. Are you ready?"**

You have read the information in this book. It should be very clear to you now that the history of the Jews, and the present situation in the Middle East are unmistakable signs that Yeshua (Jesus) is about to return to rule the world from Jerusalem. When He returns, those who are not part of God's Kingdom will be in big trouble.

Is that you ? Are you in a covenant relationship with the God of Israel? Have you made Yeshua your Lord and Messiah (saviour)? If not, I strongly suggest that you do something about your eternal situation immediately. Don't put it off until tomorrow. The Bible says that *"today is the day of salvation"*. None of us have any guarantee that we will be alive tomorrow.

If you want that covenant guarantee of eternal life in God's Kingdom, pray this prayer ....

Heavenly Father,
I acknowledge that I am a sinner in need of a saviour. I believe that Yeshua (Jesus) is the son of God, that He died on the cross and rose again on the third day. I believe that His blood seals the New Covenant which grafts me into the house of Israel and makes me a fellow citizen of Your kingdom. In return for your promise of a new and eternal life I give you my old life. I come to you today and ask that you would forgive my sin and cleanse me by the Blood of Yeshua I give you all of my heart, all of my soul, all of my mind and all of my strength. I ask that you would fill my right now with Your Holy Spirit and I ask that you would help me to fulfill the destiny and calling that you created me for.

Thank you Lord - In Yeshua's name I pray, Amen.

Appendices

Appendix 1

Another View - The Israel of God
by Lars Enerson Watchman International

WHO ARE THE ISRAEL OF GOD? This is a loaded question with very serious implications. We do not want to pretend to give a complete theological answer to this mystery, but give some input for the purpose of prayer. The question is extremely important. Identity is one of the foundational issues in life and relationships. The heresy which has been dominating the church for 1700 years, called replacement theology, was a major contributing force to one of the worst atrocities in human history: the Holocaust. Because of pride, a Gentile dominated church ignored Paul's warnings in Romans 11, and began to look down upon ethnic Israel and say, "God is finished with you! God has replaced you. We are the true Israel."

Since there is only power in the truth, the most dangerous kind of deception is always the one that looks like the truth. There is a lot of truth to the statement that the church is the true Israel We believe that a key to this theological problem is, however, to understand that the root and identity of the church is Jewish and that God has not replaced or rejected natural Israel! God has only one people: Israel! Already in the Old Testament we clearly see that there were two groups in Israel, those who believed and those who did not believe. Only those who believed entered the promised land.

A SLOW COMING

In Elijah's time God called those in Israel who worshipped God 'the remnant'. Abraham was promised both a heavenly and an earthly seed by God. *"And so from this one man, and he as good as dead, came descendants as numerous as the stars in the sky ……."* (Hebrews 11:12)

Many times Christians think that the old covenant was given to Israel and the new covenant to the church. This is not true. Both the old and the new covenants were made to Israel and with Israel.

Paul writes, *"my brothers, those of my own race, the people of Israel. Theirs is the adoption as sons; theirs the divine glory, the covenants, the receiving of the law, the temple worship* (Literally: 'the service', there is nothing mentioned about the temple in the Greek text.) *and the promises."* (Romans 9:3,4) The covenants belong to Israel. This is how Paul expresses it in the book of Ephesians, *"Therefore, remember that formerly you who are Gentiles by birth and called "uncircumcised" by those who call themselves "the circumcision" (that done in the body by the hands of men) remember that at that time you were separate from Christ, excluded from citizenship in Israel and foreigners to the covenants of the promise, without hope and without God in the world. But now in Christ Jesus you who once were far away have been brought near through the blood of Christ."*

In reading this, then, you will be able to understand my insight into the mystery of Christ. This mystery is that through the gospel the Gentiles are heirs together with Israel, members together of one body, and sharers together in the promise in Christ Jesus. (Ephesians 2:11-13; 3:4,6) Through the gospel Gentiles are heirs together with Israel.

This is far from having replaced Israel. We used to be far away, meaning far away from Israel and the covenants and the promises, but now we have come near. Through faith in the Messiah of Israel, Gentiles are cut off from their wild olive tree, and contrary to nature, grafted into the cultivated olive tree, which is Israel. God actually does not have two people, only one! The Gospel and the Church are both Jewish and belong to the Jewish people.

The Church is not a parenthesis in God's program with mankind, and Israel has no separate destiny apart from the Church!
 The Church, the bride of Messiah, is God's ultimate goal for creation! In this bride, pictured in the book of Revelation as the new Jerusalem, Gentiles *are no longer foreigners and aliens, but fellow citizens with God's people and members of God's household, built on the foundation of the apostles And prophets, with Christ Jesus himself as the chief cornerstone."* (Ephesians 2:19-20)

On the gates to this city are written the twelve tribes of Israel and on the foundation stones of the wall are written the names of the twelve Jewish apostles of Jesus. It is one family of faith, the bride of Messiah, the new Jerusalem where there is no division and separation between Jew and Gentile!

According to Hebrews Chapter 11, we are joint heirs with Abel, Enoch, Noah, Abraham, Isaac, Jacob, Joseph, Moses, Rahab, Gideon, Barak, Samson, Jephthah, David, Samuel and the prophets. *"All these people were still living by faith when they died. They did not receive the things promised; they only saw them and welcomed them from a distance. And they admitted that they were aliens and strangers on earth. They were all commended for their faith, yet none of them received what had been promised. God planned something better for us so that only together with us would they be made perfect."* (Heb 11:13, 39-40)

Even if after a few centuries there were hardly any Jews left in the Church it could never change the root and true identity of the Church. There is tremendous inherent power in the truth. Two thousand years of anti-Semitic history and false teachings cannot bury it. It will come up out of the dust and grow again in the last days. The Church is made up of those who believe, both in the Old and New Testament. This is the Israel of God that we as Gentiles by grace have been grafted into. It is very important in the church to have a proper respect and gratitude towards natural, ethnic Israel. Paul says, *"If the part of the dough offered as first fruits is holy, then the whole batch is holy; if the root is holy, so are the branches. If some of the branches have been broken off and you, though a wild olive shoot, have been grafted in among the others and now share in the nourishing sap from the olive root, do not boast over those branches If you do, consider this: You do not support the root, but the root supports you."* (Romans 11:16-18)

Spiritually there is no difference between Jew and Gentile in the body of Messiah. We all have the same head that we are destined to grow up to be like, *"and have put on the new self who is being renewed to a true knowledge according to the image of the One who created him, a renewal in which there is no distinction between Greek and Jew, circumcised and uncircumcised, barbarian, Scythian, slave and free, but Christ is all, and in all."* (Colossians 3:10-11) But even though the division between Jew and Gentile is broken down in Jesus, it is important that the respect for the natural branches does not become less after they are grafted back into their own tree.

A revelation of the true identity of the church is a powerful truth with explosive consequences that must be revealed in the last days. The traditional eschatological teaching of a pre-tribulation rapture, which has been accepted among many Bible believing Christians, is built upon a separation between Israel and the Church. When this teaching was taught for the first time, which is only about 160 years ago, it was a step in the right direction from replacement theology in that it gave natural Israel a place in God's end time program. It said, "when the church, which is understood to be made up almost entirely of Gentiles, is raptured, then God will turn to Israel and save the Jews".

How can "an incomplete" Church be raptured before the natural branches have been grafted back in? This teaching has given rise to all kinds of unscriptural ideas about Israel. The church has no separate destiny from Israel. It is the Gentiles who have been grafted into Israel!

A revelation of the true identity of the church is the key to rightly understanding God's program for the end times, and what our role and response, as well as our destiny are as believers. It is absolutely foundational for both Jews and Gentiles to understand that Yeshua, the Messiah of Israel, is the chief cornerstone of God's house who has joined both together in one body. This is a mystery that must be revealed by the Holy Spirit.

ᴬᴬᴬᴬᴬᴬᴬᴬᴬᴬ

A SLOW  COMING

Appendix 2

Replacement Theology
An Article by Meg Ferrell - California, USA

Throughout the history of the Church there has been Replacement Theology. Hidden in Replacement Theology is the age-old anti-Semitic theory of eliminating the "Hebrew people of Promise" with the "Church". The depth of this schism between the Messianic and the Gentile Church exploits an ignorance in the fullness of the Hebrew scriptures and throughout Christendom false interpretation has caused much destruction to the Jewish people. What is Replacement Theology? According to Gary Hedrick, President of The Christian Jew Foundation, Replacement Theology is defined as: A system of Biblical interpretation that sees the New Testament church as the continuation of Old Testament Israel. In its role as "New Israel" or "Spiritual Israel," the Church replaces Israel in God's economy and inherits the promises (but not the judgments) God pronounced on Israel under the old dispensation. What is the history of these "People of promise", and of whom is the early church composed? How did Replacement Theology come into existence? In answering these questions, we will understand the topic of Replacement Theology and how it permeates Christianity today.

In order to understand how Israel fits into God's plan one must understand the initial covenant agreements between God and the Hebrew nation. In the first book of the Bible, Genesis, the Lord God chose a certain people to be His own. He told a man named Abraham: *Get thee out of thy country...unto a land that*

I will show thee.. I will make of thee a great nation and bless thee, and make thy name great.... And I will bless them that bless thee, and curse him that curseth thee: and in thee shall all families of the earth be blessed (Genesis 12:2-3).

With this covenant God gave the people of Israel a specific land and a specific pledge of His protection. God later told Abraham that He would establish a covenant between the physical descendants of Abraham and Himself forever. In the Book of Genesis chapter 17, God tells Abraham that every male must be circumcised, the cutting of the male fore-skin, to be kept throughout generation to generation as a lasting covenant between God and the descendants of Abraham. In the book 'Take Hold', the Abrahamic covenant of circumcision is explained as: a very appropriate sign for the covenant God made with Abraham. The fact that it was performed on the male organ of reproduction signified that the covenant was to be passed on through Abraham's descendants through Sarah...(Berkowitz 20).

God made promises with the Jewish people via Abraham. With these covenants Abraham's descendants would be set apart forever as the chosen people of God. Through the Hebrew people He would bless every nation with the coming of their Jewish Messiah. In the Book of Numbers chapter 23, verse 19 states: *God is not a human who lies or a mortal who changes his mind. When he says something, he will do it; when he makes a promise, he will fulfil it* (Stern 178). A character trait of God is that He is *Truth* (John 14:17).

The covenants between God and Abraham were irrevocable and without condition from God Himself.

A SLOW COMING

Throughout the history of the Church there has been ignorance about the Hebraic roots of the Jewish Messiah Jesus. He was born into a Jewish family and was raised in the Hebrew culture, which practiced the very early teachings of the Torah and observed the Tenach. In the Hebrew culture His name was not the Greek version "Jesus"; in fact He was known as Yeshua, Ben Yoseph, Ben David. His lineage shows Him to be a direct descendant of Abraham, which fulfilled the messianic promise God made with Abraham back in Genesis. The blessing for every nation was the finished work of Yeshua's death on the cross for the forgiveness of sin once and for all (John 3:16-17). The simple truth is that Yeshua was born into a Jewish family, and raised by Jewish parents, His ancestors were all Jewish, He lived and worshipped as a Jew, He died a Jew, and will return a Jew. Believers who pray will pray to God in the name of a Jewish man who was known as Yeshua Ben David. (Hagee 123).

The early believers of Yeshua were known as a sect of Judaism and not a separate religion better known today as Christianity. After the resurrection of Yeshua, belief in Him spread throughout Judea. With the spread of the Gospel, many Gentiles were introduced to this Jewish Messiah. As numerous Gentiles embraced the free gift of eternal life, questions regarding the practices of the Law became an issue especially requirements of Gentiles to conform to certain Jewish covenants such as circumcision (Acts 15). As the gospel spread throughout Asia the Messianic Church carried on the teachings of their forefathers. The growing Gentile church, never before obligated in the keeping of Old Testament, learned and practiced abridged requirements set before them by the disciples of Jesus (Acts 15). In the Book of Matthew, Yeshua stated He did not come to abolish the old laws and practices of His forefathers; in fact

He said, *I came to fulfil the law* (Matthew 5:17-48). Hence, the rich teachings of the Hebrew scriptures were not to be replaced.

The Messianic promise, which was fulfilled by Yeshua, brought freedom from sin and a new relationship with God (Jeremiah 32:31-34). Yeshua never intended to change the original covenant made by God, He came to complete it.

So how did the shift take place from a dominant Jewish church to that of Gentile? The change historically was very expeditious. The Jewish place of worship in those days was the Temple in Jerusalem. Taken from the pages of "Introducing Jewish people to their Messiah" it is explained this way: As we look at history, we see that Jerusalem was the center of belief in Yeshua until AD 70, when Jerusalem was destroyed by Titus and the Diaspora began in earnest. At that time, and after the last Jewish struggle for independence in AD 130-135 the Jewish people (including believers) were dispersed and Rome became the center of faith. So with the change of the religious headquarters, the church became predominantly Gentile in nature, with the Messiah's Hebraic roots vanishing quickly throughout early Christendom.

Rome became the center of this shift. Yeshua, now known as a Roman-Greco Christ, "was removed historically and culturally from His Jewish setting, taking on the trappings of whatever society in which His message was preached". Yeshua, who once said that He had come to preach to the lost sheep of Israel (Matthew 10:6), was now stripped of His Hebrew culture and identity.

Consequently, the evolving church was now almost illiterate with regards to Jewish customs and culture. Newer Christians were regaled with false interpretations, which allowed anti-Semitism to flourish. A direct quote by Chrysostom, Patriarch of Constantinople (AD 344-407), an early leader of the church, states: "Jews are the most worthless of men - they are lecherous, greedy, rapacious ... they worship the devil. It is incumbent on all Christians to hate Jews". Historically, from statements such as this, replacement theology was well on its way in permeating the very foundations of the early Christian church. Every time false interpretations are perceived as truth it builds a counterfeit foundation based on distorted scripture. Replacement Theology has an ongoing anti-Semitic sentiment, which has continued through the ages. Throughout the crusades, which were thought to be a pious undertaking for God, Jews who were unwilling to submit to baptism were put to death. Many Jewish people were burned, beaten, and crucified on a cross as onlookers yelled "CHRIST KILLERS!" In AD 1099, crusaders in Jerusalem burnt the temple to the ground with the Jews of the city inside. While the temple burned, the crusaders "marched around the synagogue chanting hymns"

Further historical documentation of Replacement Theology can be read in the words of Martin Luther, the father and noted hero of the Protestant Reformation. At first he claimed the Jewish people to be "in-laws, blood related, and cousins". But when they did not join Luther in his assault on the Roman Church, Luther said: "All the Blood kindred of Christ burn in Hell, and they are rightly served, even according to their own words they spoke to Pilate". Luther printed up vicious and hateful statements in his tract "On the Jews and Their Lies." In this tract Luther asserts "Know this, Christian, you have no greater enemy than the Jew". Luther also entreated action against the Jewish people: [He] demanded that their synagogues be burned to the ground, their books destroyed, their homes laid waste, their cash and treasure of silver and gold be taken from them, their rabbis be forbidden to teach, and "their tongues be cut out from their throats".

It is no wonder that Hitler loved Luther's teachings. Luther was a prominent authority advocating some of the very principles of Hitler's ideology. Luther and others helped give Hitler the necessary endorsement to set in motion the mass genocide of millions of Jews. In the pages of recent history, Hitler's beliefs have been spoken out against the Jewish people. Reverend Stan Rittenhouse, a contributor to the pro-Hitler Christian Defense League Newspaper, is quoted at a Senate Foreign Relations Committee concerning Jerusalem: "Ever since the coming of Jesus Christ the Messiah, and the rejection of Christ by Israel and the Jews, God has no longer been dealing with this particular nation and race. When Christ returns, according to the Bible, He will utterly and totally destroy Israel and Jerusalem".

The sounds of Nazi concentration camps echo through the remarks of people like Reverend Rittenhouse who hold to the delusion of Replacement Theology. Looking ahead into the present, much prejudice and false interpretations of scripture exists as a result of Replacement Theology. A recent article of the Levitt Letter, author Zola Levitt, a noted Bible teacher and speaker, discusses the many fallacies of a book being used in many seminaries and Bible colleges throughout the United States today. He states, "I'm downright amazed that the obvious errors in the book are being ignored by these administrators, and that they go on teaching what they know to be wrong. The book teaches Replacement Theology and is anti-Israel and anti-Semitic".

A SLOW 🚂 COMING

Our future church leaders being taught from books noted to be anti-Semitic and anti-Israel is more than a slight problem. Replacement Theology goes against the foundation of the Church and the very scriptures it was founded upon. In Frank Eilkor's book, A time for Trumpets and not Piccolos, the author so adamantly states: "but anti-Semitism is first of all, not a Jewish problem. It is a Gentile problem...left unchallenged, anti-Semitism is a disgrace to the Christian Church and flies in the face of our claiming to be a moral force."

Regarding the Jews, has the Church been a "moral force" or has it been a "mortal farce" throughout Christendom? Jesus said that what we have done to the least of His brethren, we have done to Him (Matthew 25:40). Replace-ment Theology causes pride, arrogance, and false interpretations of the commands of God. Every Bible believing Christian, with fear and trembling must check their hearts to see if the love of God is in them concerning Israel and the Jews. Throughout the New Testament, God's plan for Israel is addressed.

Jesus states to the disciples as He sends them out, 'Go not into the way of the Gentiles, ...But go rather to the lost sheep of the house of Israel (Matthew 10:5-6 KJV). His own received Him not, as prophesied in the Old Testament Isaiah 53:3, fulfilled in John 1:11). God then opened the door for the gentile nations to receive the message of Christ. Paul, speaking to the Gentile Church with regards to Israel states: "God has not cast away His people which He foreknew" (Romans 11:20 KJV). He reminds the gentiles that God's purpose for the Jewish people to reject the message of the Gospel was that God had allowed a time for the Gentile believers to be "grafted in" (Romans 11). The grafted branches were never to take the place of the original Jewish branches. The grafted in branches are known as "a *wild olive tree*" (Romans 11:17). The Gentile nations, allowed to be grafted into the Hebraic tree, fulfilled the promise that God gave to Abraham regarding the Messiah, "*All Nations will be blessed by thee...*" (Genesis 12:2-3).

God, in His economy, has a plan for the Messianic and Gentile Church today. Jesus states in John 17:21 as He is praying to His Father, "that they may all be one. Just as you, Father, are united with me and I with you, I pray that they may be united with us, so that the world may believe that you sent me." We are to be a united force allowing cultural differences. When the world, both Jew and Gentile, see the love that we have for Jesus and for one another, the Church will be a moral force. The very commands and teachings of Jesus in Matthew 22:37-39 will show through: "You are to love Adonai your God with all your heart, with all your soul, with all your strength and with all your understanding ... and your neighbour as yourself". The Church, untied as one, would bring the love of God to a dying world, which would see their need to call upon the One that came to bring true peace and unity.

In conclusion, we can see how Replacement Theology has distorted the truth of the scriptures throughout history and even in the Church today. The covenants that God made with Abraham are to remain forever. The Messianic and Gentile believers are to be one Church created by the finished work of our Messiah. As the Church matures in the understanding of scripture and embraces its Hebrew roots, the richness of our heritage will impact the world. Not only will we be blessed as the Lord states in Genesis, He generously gives us a greater understanding into His scripture. The Lord's purpose and plans will prevail, and understanding this sooner than later saves much frustration when reading His word.

A SLOW COMING

Those who hold on to this false doctrine will have to answer this one question, as Gary Hedrick states: "The greatest weakness of Replacement Theology is its failure to address the issue of God's promises to Israel. Over and over again in the Old Testament, God (through the prophets) spoke of the future physical and spiritual restoration of Israel."

Now you can allegorize and spiritualize these passages all you want, but sooner or later every honest reader must confront this one, simple question: Did God mean what He said, or not?

In answering this one question, the reader has the responsibility to test and see if replacement theology is part of his or her biblical interpretation. Finishing with the words of Genesis 12:3, "*I will bless them that bless thee…*" we are reminded that God is not like man who can change His mind especially with His chosen people, His beloved, Israel.

Bibliography

Holy Bible. King James Version. Cambridge:
Eiklor, Frank. *A Time for Trumpets not Piccolos*! Action Against Anti-Semitism:
A Call to Christian Conscience. Orange, Ca.: Promise Publishing Company, 1988.
Introducing the Jewish People to Their Messiah. Orangeburg, NY: American Board of Missions to the Jews Publishing Company, 1977.
Stern, David. *Complete Jewish Bible Translation*. Jewish Testament Publications Inc., 1998 Clarksville, Maryland
Berkowitz, Ariel, and Dvorah Berkowitz. *Take Hold. Embracing our Divine Inheritance with Israel*. First Fruits of Zion Publishing,

Litlleton Colorado
Levitt, Zola. *Bible-teaching Ministry and Replacement Theology*
Levitt Letter. Volume 20, Number 8 August,
Hagee, John. *Final Dawn over Jerusalem*. Thomas Nelson,
Inc. Publishers, 1998. Nashville

****

Appendix 3

Chronicle of Anti-Semitism in England 1144 – 1290

1144 NORWICH - Blood libel - ritual murder accusation
1168 GLOUCESTER - Blood libel
1181 BURY ST EDMUNDS - Blood libel
1188 Saladin Tithe for Crusade - ¼ Jewish Property
1189 LONDON - Coronation of Richard Lionheart
- No Jews or women admitted to Westminster Hall
- Several Jews beaten or trampled to death
- Riots: 30 dead including Rabbi Jacob of Orleans
1190 LYNN - "pogrom" - Jews exterminated
STANFORD - Crusaders killed Jews
YORK - over 150 Jews die in Clifford's Tower
BURY ST. EDMONDS - Palm Sunday 57 Jews
massacred
DARTMOUTH - European fleet assembled: 3rd
Crusade
1194 Richard captured - Jews apportion tax for ransom
at Northampton
1210-13 BRISTOL - heavy tax on Jews : defaulters
imprisoned in castle
1215 Civil War - London : Jewry demolished
Magna Carta discriminates against Jews
1218 Jewish badge to be worn (Royal decree)
1222 Jews forbidden to build new synagogues
1231 LEICESTER - Jews expelled (Simon de Montfort)
1233 Statute of April 4th expels/imprisons all Jews unless
they serve the King
1234 NEWCASTLE - Jews expelled
1236 SOUTHAMPTON - Jews expelled

1237 NORTHAMPTONSHIRE - Jews expelled
1240 WORCESTER - Parliament of Jews to share out tax
1242 BERKHAMSTED - Jews expelled
1255 Jews mortgaged to Richard of CORNWALL :
LIONEL - blood libel
1263 LONDON - 400 Jews massacred (Palm Sunday)
WINCHESTER - Jewry plundered
1274 Jews taxed - ? property again
1275 Statutum de Judeismo - money lending at interest
forbidden
BRISTOL - Jewry burned
MARLBOROUGH, GLOUCESTER, WORCESTER,
CAMBRIDGE, GUILDFORD - Jews expelled
1277 NORTHAMPTON - Jews dragged to death by cart
horses
1278 LONDON - 680 Jews imprisoned in Tower : 290
hanged
1286 EXETER - Synod enforced all limitations against Jews
1290 LONDON - Expulsion of Jews decreed by king in
council (July 18th - ninth of Av)
All Jews to leave England before Feast of All Saints
November 1st

"The final tragedy of 1290 was the first general expulsion of
the Jews from any country in the medieval period"
- Roth: History of the Jews in England

****

Appendix 4

Comparison of Canon Law and Nazi Measures

Canonical Law	Nazi Measure
Prohibition of intermarriage and of sexual intercourse between Christians and Jews, Synod of Elvira, 306	Law for the Protection of German Blood and Honor, September 15, 1935 (RGB 1 I, 1146).
Jews and Christians not permitted to eat together, Synod of Elvira, 306.	Jews barred from dining cars (Transport Minister to Interior Minister, December 30, 1939, Document NG-3995).
Jews not allowed to hold public office, Synod of Clermont, 535	Law for the Re-establishment of the Professional Civil Service, April 7, 1933 (RGBI I, 175).
Jews not allowed to employ Christian servants or possess Christian slaves, Synod Orleans, 538.	Law for the Protection of German Blood and Honor, September 15 935 (RGBI 1 1146)

Jews not permitted to show themselves in the street during Passion Week, 3rd Synod of Orleans, 538.	Decree authorizing local authorities to bar Jews from the streets on certain days (i.e. Nazi holidays December 3, 1933 (RGB1 1 676)
Burning of the Talmud and other books, 12th Synod of Toledo, 681	Book burnings in Nazi Germany
Christians not permitted to patronize Jewish doctors, Trulanic Synod, 692.	Decree of July 25, 1938 (RGB I, 1, 969).
Christians not permitted to live in Jewish homes, Synod of Narbonne 1050	Directive by Goring providing for concentration of Jews in houses. December 28, 1938 (Borman to Rosenburg, January 17th 1939)
Jews obliged to pay taxes for support of church to the same extent as Christians, Synod of Gerona, 1078.	The "Sozialausgleichsabgabe' which provided that Jews pay a special income tax in lieu of donations for Party purposes imposed on Nazis, December 24, 1940 (RGBI I, 1666).
Jews not permitted to be plaintiffs or witnesses against Christians in the courts, 3rd Lateran Council, 1179, Canon 26	Proposal by the Party Chancellery that Jews not be permitted to institute civil suits, September 9, 942 (Bormann to Justice Ministry September 9, 1942, (NG-151)

Jews not permitted to withhold inheritance from descendants who accepted Christianity, 3d Lateran Council, 1179, Canon 26.	Decree empowering the Justice Ministry to void wills offending the "sound judgment of the people" July 31, 1938 (RGBl 1, 547).
The marking of Jewish clothes with a badge 4th Lateian Council, 1215, Canon 68. (Copied from the legislation by the Caliph Omar II [634-44] who had decreed that all Christians wear blue belts, and the Jews, yellow belts.)	Decree of September 1, 1941 (RGB1 1,547).
Construction of new synagogues prohibited, Council of Oxford, 1222.	Destruction of synagogues in entire Reich, November 10, 1938 (Heydrich to Goring, November II, 1938, PS-3058).
Christians not permitted to attend Jewish ceremonies, Synod of Vienna, 1267.	Friendly relations with Jews prohibited, October 24, 1941 (Gestapo directive, L-15).
Jews not permitted to dispute with simple Christian people about the tenets of the Catholic religion. Synod of Vienna, 1267.	Compulsory ghettoes, Synod of Breslau, 1267. Order by Heydrich, September 21 1939 (PS-3363)

Jews not permitted to sell or rent real estate to Jews, Synod of Ofen, 1279.	Decree providing for compulsory sale of real estate, December 3, 1938 (RGB II, 1709)
Adoption by a Christian of the Jewish religion or return by a Baptised Jew to the Jewish religion deigned as heresy. Synod of Mainz, 1310	Adoption by a Christian of the Jewish religion places him in jeopardy of being treated as a Jew Decision by Oberlandesgericht Konigsberg, 4th Zivilsenat, June 26, 1942 (*Die Judenfrage { Vert- rauliche Beilage}* November 1, 1942 pp 82–83)
Jews not permitted to act as agent in the conclusion of contracts between Christians, especially marriage contracts Council of Base I,	Decree of July 6, 1938 providing for liquidation of Jewish real estate agencies, brokerage agencies, and marriage agencies catering to non-Jews (RGB II, 823).
Jews not permitted to obtain academic degrees, Council of Basel, 1434, Sessio XIX	Law against Overcrowding of German Schools and Universities, April 25, 1933 (RGBI I, 225).

Appendix 5

Professions of Faith Extracted From Jews on Baptism

Visigothic Professions (early 7th centur) Of   Recceswinth, from
Leg. Vis. 12.2.J7.

To our most merciful and tranquil lord Recceswinth the King,
from us the Jews of Toledo, as witnessed or signed below. We
well remember how we were long and rightly constrained to
sign this Declaration promising in the name of King Chinthila's
holy memory to support the Catholic faith; and we have done
so. However, because our pertinacious lack of faith and the
ancient errors of our fathers held us back from believing wholly
in Our Lord Jesus Christ or accepting the Catholic truth with all
our hearts, we therefore make these promises to your greater
glory. on behalf both of ourselves and our wives and children,
through this our Declaration, undertaking for the future not to
become involved in any Jewish rites or customs nor to associate
with the accursed Jews who remain unbaptised. We will not
follow our habit of contracting incestuous unions or practising
fornication with our own relatives to the sixth degree. We will
not on any pretext, either ourselves, our children or our
descendants, choose wives from our own race; but in the case
of both sexes we will always link ourselves in matrimony with
Christians. We will not practise carnal circumcision, or celebrate
the Passover, the Sabbath or the other feast days connected
with the Jewish religion.

We will not keep to our old habit of discrimination in the matter
of food. We will do none of the things which the evil tradition of
long custom and intercourse urges upon us as Jews. Instead,
with utter faith and grace in our hearts, and with complete

devotion towards Christ the Son of the Living God, as the apostolic tradition enjoins, shall we believe on Him and confess Him.

Every custom of the holy Christian religion, feast days, marriage, and what is lawful to eat, indeed every ceremony thereof, we shall faithfully hold and embrace with all our hearts, reserving no hint within ourselves of resistance, no suspicion of deception, whereby we may come to repeat those errors we now deny, or fulfil with little or no sincerity that which we now promise to do. With regard to swines' flesh we promise to observe this rule, that if through long custom we are hardly able to eat it, we shall not through fastidiousness or error refuse the things that are cooked with it. And if in all the matters touched on above we are found in any way to transgress, either presuming to work against the Christian Faith, or promising in words to perform actions suitable to the Catholic religion, and in our deeds deferring their performance, we swear by that same Father, Son and Holy Ghost, who is One God in Three, that whoever of us is found to transgress shall either perish by the hands of our fellows, by burning or stoning, or if your splendid piety shall have spared our lives, we shall at once lose our liberty and you shall give us along with all our property to whomever you please into perpetual slavery, or dispose of us in any other manner that seems good to you.

To this end you have free authority, not only on account of your royal power, but also arising out of the stipulations of this our guarantee. This Declaration is given at Toledo in the name of the Lord, on the 18th of February in the sixth year of your glorious reign.

A SLOW  COMING

Appendix 6

Fuller Theological Seminary News Release

PASADENA, CALIFORNIA Dean Arthur F. Glasser and the School of World Mission faculty of Fuller Theological Seminary have released the following statement: "We of the School of World Mission faculty of Fuller Theological Seminary feel constrained to address ourselves and the Church at large concerning the Jewish people. Particularly so at this time when the third commonwealth of Israel is celebrating its 28th anniversary and when we find ourselves much in prayer that the Jewish presence in the Middle East shall become under God an instrument for reconciliation and peace.

"We are profoundly grateful for the heritage given to us by the Jewish people which is so vital for our own Christian faith. We believe that God used the Jewish people as the sole repository of the history centered disclosure of himself to mankind. This revelation began with Abraham and continued to the Jewish writers of the New Testament. Not only were the oracles of God committed to them (Romans 3:2), but it was through this people that God chose to bring Jesus Christ into the world. We believe that he is the only hope of salvation for the Jewish people, and for all mankind. Indeed, we continue to pray that through the mercy and blessing of God, the Jewish people shall turn to the Messiah Jesus and become once again a light to the nations that his salvation may reach to the end of the earth (Isaiah. 49:6).

194

"We wish to charge the Church, as a whole, to do more than merely include the Jewish people in their evangelistic outreach. We would encourage an active response to the mandate of Romans 1:16 calling for evangelism "to the Jew first." For this we have the precedent of a great Jewish missionary, the Apostle Paul. Though sent to the Gentile world, he never relinquished his burden for his own kinsmen after the flesh. Wherever he travelled, he first visited the synagogue before presenting Christ to the Gentiles. So it must be in every generation. We must provide a priority opportunity for our Jewish friends to respond to the Messiah. They are our benefactors and it was they who first evangelised us. Furthermore, the Gospel we share with them must be carried to all tribes and peoples and tongues.

"We regret exceedingly that Christians have not always shared this Gospel with the Jewish people in a loving and ethical manner. Too often, while interested in Jewish evangelism in general, we have demeaned the dignity of the Jewish person by our unkind stereotyping and our disregard for Jewish sensitivities. How un-Christlike we have been!

"Likewise, we have unwittingly encouraged Jewish converts to divest themselves of their Jewish heritage and culture. For this too, we would repent and express our regret that the Western influence on our beliefs has precluded the original Jewish context. Our Church is culturally and spiritually poorer for it.

"In our day we are encouraged that thousands of Jewish people are coming to the Messiah. This being so, we cannot but call upon the Christian community to renew its commitment to share lovingly the Gospel of Jesus with the Jewish people. And we heartily encourage Jewish believers in him, including those who call themselves Messianic Jews, Hebrew-Christians, and Jews for Jesus, to retain their Jewish heritage, culture, religious practices and marriage customs within the context of a sound Biblical theology expressing Old and New Testament truth. Their freedom in Christ to do this cannot but enrich the Church in our day.

"More we feel it incumbent on Christians in all traditions to reinstate the work of Jewish evangelism in their missionary obedience. Jewish-oriented programs should be developed. Appropriate agencies for Jewish evangelism should be formed. And churches everywhere should support those existing institutions which are faithfully and lovingly bearing a Christian witness to the Jewish people."

Pasadena, California   May 12, 1976

Appendix 7

The Willowbank Declaration
On the Christian Gospel and the Jewish People

Romans 1:16 *"The Gospel is the power of God for salvation, to everyone who believes, to the Jew first and also to the Greek."*

Romans 10:1 *"Brethren, my heart's desire and prayer to God for Israel is that they may be saved."*

PREAMBLE Every Christian must acknowledge an immense debt of gratitude to the Jewish people. The Gospel is the good news that Jesus is the Christ, the long-promised Jewish Messiah, who by his life, death and resurrection saves from sin and all its consequences. Those who worship Jesus as their Divine Lord and Saviour have thus received God's most precious gift through the Jewish people. Therefore they have compelling reason to show love to that people in every possible way.

Concerned about humanity everywhere, we are resolved to up hold the right of Jewish people to a just and peaceful existence everywhere, both in the land of Israel and in their communities throughout the world. We repudiate past persecutions of Jews by those identified as Christians, and we pledge ourselves to resist every form of anti-Semitism. As the supreme way of demonstrating this love, we seek to encourage the Jewish people, along with all other peoples, to receive God's gift of life through Jesus the Messiah and accordingly the growing number of Jewish Christians brings us great joy.

A SLOW  COMING

In making this Declaration we stand in a long and revered Christian tradition, which in 1980 was highlighted by a landmark statement, "Christian Witness to the Jewish People" issued by the Lausanne Committee for World Evangelisation. Now, at this Consultation on the Gospel and the Jewish People, sponsored by the World Evangelical Fellowship and supported by the Lausanne Cornmittee, we reaffirm our commitment to the Jewish people and our desire to share the Gospel with them.

This declaration is made in response to growing doubts and widespread confusion among Christians about the need for, and the propriety of, endeavors to share faith in Jesus Christ with Jewish people. Several factors unite to produce the uncertain state of mind that the Declaration seeks to resolve.

The holocaust, perpetrated as it was by leaders and citizens of a supposedly "Christian nation" has led to a sense in some quarters that Christian credibility among Jews has been totally destroyed. Accordingly, some have shrunk back from addressing the Jewish people with the Gospel.

Some who see the creation of the State of Israel as a direct fulfilment of Biblical prophecy have concluded that the Christian task at this time is to "comfort Israel" by supporting this new political entity, rather than to challenge Jews by direct evangelism. Some church leaders have retreated from embracing the task of evangelising Jews as a responsibility of Christian mission.
Rather, a new theology is being embraced which holds that God's covenant with Israel through Abraham establishes all Jews in God's favour for all times, and so makes faith in Jesus Christ for salvation needless so far as they are concerned.

198

On this basis, it is argued that dialogue with Jews in order to understand each other better, and cooperation in the quest for socio-economic shalom is all that Christian mission requires in relation to the Jewish people. Continued attempts to do what the Church has done from the first, in seeking to win Jews to Jesus as Messiah, are widely opposed and decried by Christian as well as Jewish leaders.

Attempts to bring Jews to faith in Jesus are frequently denounced as proselytising. This term is often used to imply dishonest and coercive modes of inducement, appeal to unworthy motives, and disregard of the question of truth even though it is truth that is being disseminated.

In recent years, Messianic Jewish believers in Jesus who as Christians celebrate and maximize their Jewish identity have emerged as active evangelists to the Jewish community. Jewish leaders often accused them of deception on the grounds that one cannot be both a Jew and a Christian. While these criticisms may reflect Judaism's current effort to define itself as a distinct religion in opposition to Christianity, they have led to much bewilderment and some misunderstanding and mistrust.

The Declaration responds to this complex situation and seeks to set directions for the future according to the Scriptures.

****

A SLOW COMING

NO PALESTINIAN STATE

In March 1971 the Dutch newspaper Trouw published an interview with Palestine Liberation Organization (PLO) executive committee member Zahir Muhsein. Here's what he said. "The Palestinian people do not exist. The creation of a Palestinian state is only a means for continuing our struggle against the state of Israel and for our Arab unity. In reality, today there is no difference between Jordanians, Palestinians, Syrians, and Lebanese. Only for political and tactical reasons do we speak today about the existence of a Palestinian people.

"For tactical reasons, Jordan, which is a sovereign state with de-fined borders, cannot raise claims to Haifa and Jaffa, while as a Palestinian, I can undoubtedly demand Haifa, Jaffa, Beersheva and Jerusalem. However, the moment we reclaim our right to all of Palestine, we will wait not even a minute to unite Palestine and Jordan."

BRITISH PARTITION MAP

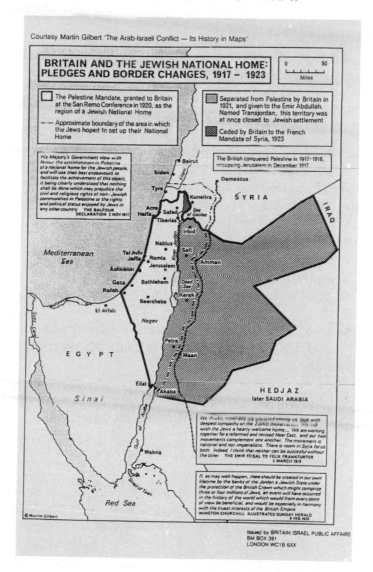

Courtesy Martin Gilbert 'The Arab-Israeli Conflict — Its History in Maps'

BRITAIN AND THE JEWISH NATIONAL HOME: PLEDGES AND BORDER CHANGES, 1917 – 1923

A SLOW  COMING

About OUT of ZION
Ministries

"A LIGHT TO THE NATIONS"

Isaiah 49:6 *Is it too small a thing that you should be my servant; To raise up the tribes of Jacob; And to restore the preserved ones of Israel; I will also give you as light to the Nations*

****

- A Ministry in keeping with Romans 1:16, taking the Gospel to the Jew first and also to the Gentiles.

- Sharing with the Church about her Biblical roots and her relationship and responsibility to Israel and the Jewish people.

- Awakening the Church to the prophetic relevance of the restoration of Israel and the Messianic Movement.

Introducing Out of Zion Ministries

Out of Zion focuses on the above three areas. Since the early days of the ministry, David and Josie have seen the Lord miraculously open doors for them to travel to many different nations, to minister in these key areas.

1/ Evangelism to the Jew First (Romans 1:16)

Out of Zion partners with other Believers to help organize Jewish music and dance festivals in Central Asia. The fruit of these festivals is the hundreds of Jews who have come to know the God of their forefathers and to accept Yeshua as their Messiah.

A number of the Jewish people who were saved at Out of Zion outreach festivals now live in Israel and many of the others are members of the 3 Messianic congregations that were planted in Kazakstan, Krygestan and Uzbekistan.

2/ Evangelism to the Nations

David is now sensing the time is right for Messianic Jews to fulfill the age old call on the Jewish people, to be *a light to the Nations.* Specifically to take the Word of the Lord out from Zion to the Nations. (Isaiah 2:3)

In May 2000 David preached the Gospel in Samoa. More than 116 people came to the Lord at the 3 outreach meetings. In May 2001, David preached in Nellore, India. Over the 3 night Gospel festival, more than 300 people made first time confessions of faith in Yeshua.

In 2001, there was a series of outreach meetings sponsored by the FGBMI in Malaysia. There is nothing more Biblical. than a Jew, taking the message about the King of the Jews to the peoples of the world.

A SLOW  COMING

Sharing with the Church

In 1997 David sensed the Lord directing him to dedicate the majority of his time to take the message of the Jewish roots of Christianity to the Church. It is hoped that as Christians begin to understand their Biblical relationship to Israel and the Jewish people, they will also begin to understand their responsibility to work alongside the Lord as He fulfills His prophesied restoration of Israel.

"Hasten the Day of His Coming" - 2 Peter 3:12

How many times have you heard it said, "We are living in exciting times" ? Probably so many times that it may have become just another cliché. However, if you are open to the Word of the Lord, and have a heart to discern what He is doing in your midst, that statement becomes real and the Lord's promised return begins to appear very near.

Acts 3:21 tells us that the Lord will not come back until all of the ancient prophecies have been fulfilled. These prophecies concern the restoration of Israel and the Jewish people. In Ezekiel 36 and 37, we see that the Lord is working on three tracks, the restoration of the land, the physical restoration of the Jewish people to the land, and ultimately their spiritual restoration of their Messiah (David their King Hosea 3:5). Since 1948, these 3000 year old prophecies have been, and are continuing to be amazingly fulfilled before our very eyes.

We have the privilege of having come to God's kingdom "for such a time as this". The Lord is at work fulfilling His word.

1 Corinthians 3:9 describes us as "God's fellow workers" and 2

Peter 3:12 indicates that we can actually hasten the day of the Lord's coming. How do we do this? - By aligning ourselves with His plans and purposes for Israel and the Jewish people.

We believe that the scriptures clearly teach that the Lord has called the Gentiles to assist Him in bringing home the scattered sheep of the House of Israel, physically (Isaiah 49:22), and also spiritually (Romans 11:11, Is 62:11)

Romans 1:16 says that the gospel is for the Jewish people first. Josie and I encourage you to get involved. Seek the Lord as to what specific area and how He would have you utilize the "first fruit" of your life. If you feel that it is not for you to become involved personally, then you can still be obedient to this call by partnering with a ministry that does minister to the Jewish people. We encourage you to become involved, prayerfully and financially in the restoration of Israel, thus hastening the day of the Lord's return.

The Lord bless you as you bless the descendants of Abraham through prayer and practical support.

Please Contact us :

If your congregation would like to host an **Out of Zion** speaker or seminar

If you wish to receive the **Out of Zion** bi-monthly newsletter or weekly Carmel Alert news report

If you wish to make a contribution to **Out of Zion** Ministries

OUT of ZION Ministries

Mt. Carmel
Haifa.
ISRAEL.

Email: kiwi@netvision.net.il
Website: www.out-of-zion.com

The Silver Family

David, Josie, Jordan and Stefan